AF696846

CPCU 500 Course Guide

Foundations of Risk Management and Insurance
1st Edition

The Institutes
720 Providence Road, Suite 100
Malvern, Pennsylvania 19355-3433

Unless otherwise apparent, examples used in The Institutes materials related to this course are based on hypothetical situations and are for educational purposes only. The characters, persons, products, services, and organizations described in these examples are fictional. Any similarity or resemblance to any other character, person, product, services, or organization is merely coincidental. The Institutes are not responsible for such coincidental or accidental resemblances.

This material may contain Internet Web site links external to The Institutes. The Institutes neither approve nor endorse any information, products, or services to which any external Web sites refer. Nor do The Institutes control these Web sites' content or the procedures for Web site content development.

The Institutes specifically disclaim any implied warranties of merchantability or fitness for a particular purpose. No warranty may be created or extended by sales representatives or written sales materials.

The Institutes materials related to this course are provided with the understanding that The Institutes are not engaged in rendering legal, accounting, or other professional service. Nor are The Institutes explicitly or implicitly stating that any of the processes, procedures, or policies described in the materials are the only appropriate ones to use. The advice and strategies contained herein may not be suitable for every situation.

1st Edition • 2nd Printing • October 2010

ISBN 978-0-89463-418-5

Contents

Study Materials Available for CPCU 500

Foundations of Risk Management and Insurance, 1st ed., 2010, AICPCU.

CPCU 500 *Course Guide*, 1st ed., 2010, AICPCU. (includes access code for SMART Online Practice Exams).

CPCU 500 SMART Study Aids—Review Notes and Flash Cards, 1st ed.

Student Resources

Catalog A complete listing of our offerings can be found in *Succeed,* The Institutes' professional development catalog, including information about:

- Current programs and courses
- Current textbooks, course guides, SMART Study Aids, and online offerings
- Program completion requirements
- Exam registration

To obtain a copy of the catalog, visit our Web site at www.TheInstitutes.org or contact Customer Service at (800) 644-2101.

How to Prepare for Institute Exams This free handbook is designed to help you by:

- Giving you ideas on how to use textbooks and course guides as effective learning tools
- Providing steps for answering exam questions effectively
- Recommending exam-day strategies

The handbook is printable from the Student Services Center on The Institutes' Web site at www.TheInstitutes.org, or available by calling Customer Service at (800) 644-2101.

Educational Counseling Services To ensure that you take courses matching both your needs and your skills, you can obtain free counseling from The Institutes by:

- E-mailing your questions to advising@TheInstitutes.org
- Calling an Institutes' counselor directly at (610) 644-2100, ext. 7601
- Obtaining and completing a self-inventory form, available on our Web site at www.TheInstitutes.org or by contacting Customer Service at (800) 644-2101

Exam Registration Information As you proceed with your studies, be sure to arrange for your exam.

- Visit our Web site at www.TheInstitutes.org forms to access and print the Registration Booklet, which contains information and forms needed to register for your exam.
- Plan to register with The Institutes well in advance of your exam.

How to Contact the Institutes For more information on any of these publications and services:

- Visit our Web site at www.TheInstitutes.org
- Call us at (800) 644-2101 or (610) 644-2100 outside the U.S.
- E-mail us at customerservice@TheInstitutes.org
- Fax us at (610) 640-9576
- Write to us at The Institutes, Customer Service, 720 Providence Road, Suite 100, Malvern, PA 19355-3433

Using This Course Guide

This course guide will help you learn the course content and prepare for the exam.

Each assignment in this course guide typically includes the following components:

Educational Objectives These are the most important study tools in the course guide. Because all of the questions on the exam are based on the Educational Objectives, the best way to study for the exam is to focus on these objectives.

▶▶

Each Educational Objective typically begins with one of the following action words, which indicate the level of understanding required for the exam:

Analyze—Determine the nature and the relationship of the parts.

Apply—Put to use for a practical purpose.

Associate—Bring together into relationship.

Calculate—Determine numeric values by mathematical process.

Classify—Arrange or organize according to class or category.

Compare—Show similarities and differences.

Contrast—Show only differences.

Define—Give a clear, concise meaning.

Describe—Represent or give an account.

Determine—Settle or decide.

Evaluate—Determine the value or merit.

Explain—Relate the importance or application.

Identify or list—Name or make a list.

Illustrate—Give an example.

Justify—Show to be right or reasonable.

Paraphrase—Restate in your own words.

Recommend—Suggest or endorse something to be used

Summarize—Concisely state the main points.

Outline The outline lists the topics in the assignment. Read the outline before the required reading to become familiar with the assignment content and the relationships of topics.

Key Words and Phrases These words and phrases are fundamental to understanding the assignment and have a common meaning for those working in insurance. After completing the required reading, test your understanding of the assignment's Key Words and Phrases by writing their definitions.

Review Questions The review questions test your understanding of what you have read. Review the Educational Objectives and required reading, then answer the questions to the best of your ability. When you are finished, check the answers at the end of the assignment to evaluate your comprehension.

Application Questions These questions continue to test your knowledge of the required reading by applying what you've studied to "hypothetical" real-life situations. Again, check the suggested answers at the end of the assignment to review your progress.

Sample Exam Your course guide includes a sample exam (located at the back) or a code for accessing SMART Online Practice Exams (which appears on the inside back cover). Use the option available for the course you're taking to become familiar with the test format.

For courses that offer SMART Online Practice Exams, you can either download and print a sample credentialing exam or take full practice exams using questions like those that will appear on your credentialing exam. SMART Online Practice Exams are as close as you can get to experiencing an actual exam before taking one.

More Study Aids

The Institutes also produce supplemental study tools, called SMART Study Aids, for many of our courses. When SMART Study Aids are available for a course, they are listed on both page iii of this course guide and on the first page of each assignment. SMART Study Aids include Review Notes and Flash Cards and are excellent tools to help you learn and retain the information in each assignment.

CPCU Advisory Committee

F. Scott Addis, CPCU
The Addis Group

Chris Amrhein, AAI
Amrhein and Associates, Inc.

Scott A. Behrent, CPCU, AIC
Farm Family Casualty Insurance Company

Anne Crabbs, CPCU
State Auto Insurance Companies

Eric A. Fitzgerald
Marshall, Dennehey, Warner, Coleman & Goggin

Rob Galbraith, CPCU, CLU, ChFC
USAA

Dennis M. Halligan, CPCU
Farmers Group

Joseph S. Harrington, CPCU, ARP
American Association of Insurance Services

Frederick P. Hessenthaler, CPCU
Chubb & Son

Robert E. Hoyt, PhD, CLU, ChFC
University of Georgia

James Jones, CPCU, AIC, ARM, AIS
Katie School of Insurance & Financial Services

John J. Kelly, CPCU, CLU, ChFC, ARM, AAI
CPCU Society

Johannah Lipscher, CPCU, AIS
Zurich North America

Dennis F. Mahoney, CEBS, CFP
The Wharton School, University of Pennsylvania

Gregory Massey, CPCU, CIC, CRM, ARM
Zurich North America

Michael McVey, CPCU, MBA, ARe
Penn National Insurance

Claire E. Mead, CPCU, MBA, AIS, ACS
American National Property and Casualty Company

Ronald M. Metcho, CPCU, ARM, AAI
Saul-Metcho Insurance

Debra Mochi, CPCU
Marsh Inc.

Jesus Pedre, CPCU, INS, AIC, IR, AIS, AIC
Texas Department of Insurance

James E. Reagan, CPCU, AU
Farmers Mutual Fire Ins. Co. of Salem County

Brian P. Savko, CPCU
State Farm Insurance Companies

Wade E. Sheeler, CPCU
Grinnell Mutual Group

James A. Sherlock, CPCU, CLU, ARM
ACE, USA

Angela K. Sparks, CPCU
State Farm Insurance Companies

Christine A. Sullivan, CPCU, AIM
Allstate Insurance Company

Lawton Swan, CPCU, CLU, ARM, CSP, CMC
Interisk Corporation

Sean S. Sweeney, CPCU, RPLU, ARe
Phildelphia Insurance Company

Kenneth J. Swymer, Sr., EdD, CPCU
Liberty Mutual Group

Angela Viane, CPCU, AIS
Zurich North America

Direct Your Learning

ASSIGNMENT 1

Introduction to Risk Management

Educational Objectives

After learning the content of this assignment, you should be able to:

1. Describe each of the following in the context of risk:
   - Uncertainty
   - Possibility
   - Possibility compared with probability
2. Explain how the following classifications of risk apply and how they help in risk management:
   - Pure and speculative risk
   - Subjective and objective risk
   - Diversifiable and nondiversifiable risk
   - Quadrants of risk (hazard, operational, financial, and strategic)
3. Describe the three financial consequences of risk.
4. Describe the basic purpose and scope of risk management in terms of the following:
   - How risk management is practiced by individuals and organizations
   - The basic distinction between traditional risk management and enterprise-wide risk management
5. Describe the following elements for property, liability, personnel, and net income loss exposures:
   - Assets exposed to loss
   - Causes of loss, including associated hazards
   - Financial consequences of loss
6. Describe the benefits of risk management and how it reduces the financial consequences of risk for individuals, organizations, and society.

1
ASSIGNMENT

Educational Objectives, continued

7. Summarize pre-loss and post-loss risk management program goals and the conflicts that can arise as they are implemented.
8. Describe each of the steps in the risk management process.

Outline

- **Understanding and Quantifying Risk**
  - A. Uncertainty and Possibility
  - B. Possibility and Probability
- **Classifications of Risk**
  - A. Pure and Speculative Risk
  - B. Subjective and Objective Risk
  - C. Diversifiable and Nondiversifiable Risk
  - D. Quadrants of Risk: Hazard, Operational, Financial, and Strategic
- **Financial Consequences of Risk**
  - A. Expected Cost of Losses or Gains
  - B. Expenditures on Risk Management
  - C. Cost of Residual Uncertainty
- **Basic Purpose and Scope of Risk Management**
  - A. Risk Management for Individuals and Organizations
  - B. Traditional Risk Management and Enterprise-Wide Risk Management
- **Loss Exposures**
  - A. Elements of Loss Exposures
    1. Asset Exposed to Loss
    2. Cause of Loss
    3. Financial Consequences of Loss
  - B. Types of Loss Exposures
    1. Property Loss Exposures
    2. Liability Loss Exposures
    3. Personnel Loss Exposures
    4. Net Income Loss Exposures
- **Risk Management Benefits**
  - A. Reducing the Financial Consequences of Risk
  - B. Benefits to Individuals
  - C. Benefits to Organizations
  - D. Benefits to Society
- **Risk Management Program Goals**
  - A. Pre-Loss Goals
    1. Economy of Operations
    2. Tolerable Uncertainty
    3. Legality
    4. Social Responsibility
  - B. Post-Loss Goals
    1. Survival
    2. Continuity of Operations
    3. Profitability
    4. Earnings Stability
    5. Social Responsibility
    6. Growth
  - C. Conflict Between Goals
- **The Risk Management Process**
  - A. Step 1: Identifying Loss Exposures
  - B. Step 2: Analyzing Loss Exposures
  - C. Step 3: Examining the Feasibility of Risk Management Techniques
  - D. Step 4: Selecting the Appropriate Risk Management Techniques
    1. Financial Considerations
    2. Nonfinancial Considerations
  - E. Step 5: Implementing the Selected Risk Management Techniques
  - F. Step 6: Monitoring Results and Revising the Risk Management Program
    1. Establishing Standards of Acceptable Performance
    2. Comparing Actual Results With Standards
    3. Correcting Substandard Performance
    4. Evaluating Standards That Have Been Substantially Exceeded

s.m.a.r.t. tips

Don't spend time on material you have already mastered. The SMART Review Notes are organized by the Educational Objectives found in each assignment to help you track your study.

For each assignment, you should define or describe each of the Key Words and Phrases and answer each of the Review and Application Questions.

Educational Objective 1

Describe each of the following in the context of risk:

- **Uncertainty**
- **Possibility**
- **Possibility compared with probability**

Key Word or Phrase

Probability

Review Questions

1-1. Describe the two elements of risk.

1-2. Describe the difference between possibility and probability.

1-3. Explain how understanding various outcome probabilities can aid an organization in its risk management efforts.

Application Question

1-4. Atwell Bus Company, Inc. (Atwell) is a corporation providing bus transportation to public and private schools in Midland County. Atwell owns 200 new school buses. Its major competitors are two larger bus companies that operate in the same general area. School districts and private schools generally award annual contracts to the lowest bidder from among the bus companies, but they also consider overall performance and level of service in their evaluations. Explain how the following elements apply to Atwell's risks.

a. Uncertainty

b. Possibility

c. Probability

Educational Objective 2

Explain how the following classifications of risk apply and how they help in risk management:

- **Pure and speculative risk**
- **Subjective and objective risk**
- **Diversifiable and nondiversifiable risk**
- **Quadrants of risk (hazard, operational, financial, and strategic)**

Review Questions

2-1. Describe how classifying risk helps an organization's risk management process.

2-2. Explain why it is important to distinguish between speculative risks and pure risks when making risk management decisions.

2-3. Explain reasons why the assessment of subjective and objective risk might differ.

2-4. Describe how operational risks are different from strategic risks.

Application Question

2-5. Classify each of the following risks as pure or speculative, subjective or objective, and diversifiable or nondiversifiable.

a. Damage to an office building resulting from a hurricane

b. Reduction in value of retirement savings

c. Products liability claim against a manufacturer

Educational Objective 3

Describe the three financial consequences of risk.

Review Questions

3-1. Identify three components that constitute the financial consequences of risk faced by individuals or organizations.

3-2. List hidden costs that can affect an organization's calculation of expected costs of loss.

3-3. Describe the costs of residual uncertainty.

Application Question

3-4. Mary has purchased a vacation home located in a coastal region of South Florida. Give examples of each of the three financial consequences of risk that Mary is now exposed to with this purchase.

Educational Objective 4

Describe the basic purpose and scope of risk management in terms of the following:

- **How risk management is practiced by individuals and organizations**
- **The basic distinction between traditional risk management and enterprise-wide risk management**

Review Questions

4-1. Explain how risk management practices differ between individuals and organizations.

4-2. Describe the difference in scope between traditional risk management and enterprise-wide risk management.

4-3. Explain how the focus of risk management efforts differs for traditional risk management and enterprise-wide risk management.

Educational Objective 5

Describe the following elements for property, liability, personnel, and net income loss exposures:

- **Assets exposed to loss**
- **Causes of loss, including associated hazards**
- **Financial consequences of loss**

Key Words and Phrases

Loss exposure

Hazard

Moral hazard

Morale hazard (attitudinal hazard)

Physical hazard

Legal hazard

▶▶

Property loss exposure

Tangible property

Real property (realty)

Personal property

Intangible property

Liability loss exposure

Personnel loss exposure

Personal loss exposure

Net income loss exposure

Review Questions

5-1. List three elements necessary to describe a loss exposure.

5-2. Identify types of assets that could be loss exposures for the following entities.

a. Organization's assets

b. Individual's assets

5-3. Describe the four classifications of hazards.

5-4. Identify three factors that affect the financial consequences of a loss.

5-5. Distinguish between the following types of property.

a. Tangible property

b. Intangible property

c. Real property

d. Personal property

5-6. Explain how an organization or individual might experience a financial loss from the following type of loss exposures.

a. Property loss exposure

b. Liability loss exposure

c. Personnel loss exposure

d. Net income loss exposure

Application Question

5-7. ABC's Used Cars, Inc., (ABC) has applied for property and liability insurance. Describe a possible hazard that ABC might face in each of the following categories

a. Moral hazard

b. Morale hazard

c. Physical hazard

d. Legal hazard

Educational Objective 6

Describe the benefits of risk management and how it reduces the financial consequences of risk for individuals, organizations, and society.

Review Questions

6-1. Explain how expected losses and residual uncertainty are affected when an organization has an effective risk management program.

6-2. Identify the costs used to compute the overall financial consequence of risk for a given asset or activity.

6-3. Identify ways that risk management benefits each of the following entities.

a. Individuals

b. Organizations

c. Society

Educational Objective 7

Summarize pre-loss and post-loss risk management program goals and the conflicts that can arise as they are implemented.

Key Words and Phrases

Pre-loss goals

Post-loss goals

Review Questions

7-1. Describe four pre-loss operational goals supported by an effective and efficient risk management program.

7-2. List six possible post-loss goals for an organization after a significant foreseeable loss has occurred.

7-3. Identify the steps an organization might take to forestall an intolerable shutdown and ensure continuous operations after a loss occurs.

Application Question

7-4. Provide an example of how each of the following risk management program goals can conflict with the pre-loss goal of economy of operations.

a. Tolerable uncertainty

b. Legality

▶▶

c. Social responsibility

Educational Objective 8

Describe each of the steps in the risk management process.

Review Questions

8-1. List the six steps in the risk management process.

8-2. Describe four dimensions used to analyze a loss exposure.

8-3. Describe how an organization uses risk control and risk financing techniques to manage loss exposures.

8-4. Identify the forecasts an organization might use to analyze the costs of a risk management technique.

8-5. List the four steps required to monitor and revise a risk management program.

Application Question

8-6. For each of the following, suggest a standard that a risk management professional might use to gauge performance.

a. Product shipments to customers that are damaged in transit

b. Customer slip-and-fall injuries in a retail shop

c. Employees injured in warehouse activities

Answers to Assignment 1 Questions

NOTE: These answers are provided to give students a basic understanding of acceptable types of responses. They often are not the only valid answers and are not intended to provide an exhaustive response to the questions.

Educational Objective 1

1-1. The following are the two elements of risk: (1) Uncertainty of outcomes—Risk involves uncertainty about the type of outcome, the timing of the outcome, or both the type and timing of the outcome; (2) Possibility of a negative outcome—At least one of the potential outcomes is negative, which means a loss or reduction in value.

1-2. Possibility means that an outcome or event may or may not occur. It does not quantify risk; it only verifies that risk is present. Probability, the likelihood that an outcome or event will occur, quantifies risk. It is measurable and has a value between zero and one.

1-3. With an understanding of various outcome probabilities, an organization can focus its risk management efforts on risks that can be appropriately managed. The organization can also use probabilities to decide which activities (and associated risks) to undertake and which risk management techniques to use.

1-4.

a. Atwell faces uncertainty regarding which contracts it will win (what will occur) or what its risk for next year will be (when it will occur).

b. Atwell faces the possibility (may or may not happen) of a collision between two loaded school buses.

c. Because Atwell has a new fleet of buses, the probability (likelihood) of mechanical breakdown is low.

Educational Objective 2

2-1. Classification can help with assessing risks because many risks in the same classification have similar attributes. It also can help with controlling and financing risk, because many risks in the same classification can be controlled or financed with similar techniques. Classifying risk also helps with the administrative function of risk management by helping to ensure that risks in the same classifications are less likely to be overlooked.

2-2. It is important for an organization to distinguish between speculative risks and pure risks when making risk management decisions because the two types of risk are often managed differently. For example, most insurance policies are not designed to handle speculative risks.

2-3. The assessment of subjective and objective risk may differ for these reasons:

- Familiarity and control—For example, although many people consider air travel (over which they have no control) to carry a high degree of risk, they are much more likely to suffer a serious injury when driving their cars, where the perception of control is much greater.
- Severity over frequency—People often have two views of low-probability, high-consequence events. The first misconception is the "it can't happen to me" view, which is assigning a probability of zero to low-probability events such as natural disasters, murder, fires, accidents, and so on. The second misconception is overstating the probability of a low-probability event, which is common for people who have personally been exposed to the low-probability event previously. If the effect of a particular event can be severe, such as the potentially destructive effects of a hurricane or earthquake, the perception of the frequency of deaths resulting from such an event is increased. This perception may be enhanced by the increased media coverage given to high-severity events.

2-4. Operational risks are pure risks that fall outside of the traditional hazard risk category and could jeopardize service-related or manufacturing-related business functions. Strategic risks are fundamental to an organization's existence and business plan because they have a current or future effect on earnings or capital arising from adverse business decisions, improper implementation of decisions, or lack of responsiveness to changes in the industry or changes in demand.

2-5.

a. The risk of hurricane damage to an office building is a pure risk in that there is no chance of gain from the damage. The risk is both subjective and objective. The building owner may have his/her own idea about the frequency or severity of loss (subjective), and there are objective measures of frequency and severity based on historical data or catastrophe modeling. Hurricane damage to an office building is usually non-diversifiable because hurricanes affect many properties simultaneously.

b. The reduction in value to retirement savings is a speculative risk because there is a chance of loss, no loss, or gain on retirement savings. The risk is both subjective and objective. The investor may have his/her own expectations of retirement investments (subjective) as well as historical data (objective) on investment returns. The risk is diversifiable because the investor has many investment options to offset the risk of a reduction in retirement savings.

c. The risk of products liability claims against a manufacturer is a pure risk, is both subjective and objective, and is diversifiable. The manufacturer can diversify into other products or services to reduce its exposure to products liability claims.

Educational Objective 3

3-1. Three components that constitute the financial consequences of risk faced by individuals or organizations are (1) expected cost of losses or gains, (2) expenditures on risk management, and (3) cost of residual uncertainty.

▶▶

3-2. The following hidden costs can affect an organization's expected loss costs calculation:

- Time lost by the injured employee
- Time lost by other employees who stop work
- Time lost by foremen, supervisors, or other executives
- Time spent on the case by first-aid attendants and hospital department staff (when not paid by the insurer)
- Damage to the machine, tools, or other property or the spoilage of material
- Interference with production, failure to fill orders on time, loss of bonuses, payment of forfeits, and other similar causes of loss
- Continuation of the injured employee's wages after the employee returns to work even though the employee's services may temporarily be worth less than normal value
- Loss of profit on the injured employee's productivity and on the idle machines
- Lost productivity because of employees' excitement or weakened morale resulting from the accident
- Overhead per injured employee that continues while the employee is not productive

3-3. Residual uncertainty is the level of risk that remains after individuals or organizations implement their risk management programs. The cost of this uncertainty is difficult to measure but still may significantly affect the individual or organization. For individuals, the cost of residual uncertainty may include lost salary or forgone investment opportunities. For organizations, the cost of residual uncertainty includes the effect that uncertainty has on consumers, investors, and suppliers. For example, suppliers may be less willing to sell supplies on credit to organizations with large amounts of residual uncertainty.

3-4. Examples of each of the three financial consequences of risk that Mary now faces include the following:

- Expected cost of gain or loss—Based on her new home's exposure to loss from fire, flood, and hurricane damage (among other causes of loss), Mary can expect to suffer losses to both the real property (the building and land) and to any personal property in the house.
- Expenditures on risk management—Mary may choose to install hurricane shutters, hurricane roof straps, and other risk control items to reduce the amount of loss that may occur during a hurricane. Mary will also purchase homeowners insurance on the property.
- Cost of residual uncertainty—Mary now has uncertainty regarding the causes, frequency, and severity of loss to her new property. Although her risk control efforts can mitigate any losses and she has purchased homeowners insurance, Mary will still have some uninsured costs associated with any loss.

Educational Objective 4

4-1. Individuals and families often practice risk management informally (purchasing insurance policies and contributing to savings plans) without explicitly following a risk management process. In smaller organizations, risk management is not usually a dedicated function, but one of many tasks carried out by the owner or senior manager. In many larger organizations, the risk management function is conducted as part of a formalized risk management program.

4-2. The scope of traditional risk management is on losses generated by pure, as opposed to speculative, risks.

The scope of enterprise-wide risk management encompasses all types of risk with the intent of maximizing the organization's value.

4-3. Traditional risk management focuses on managing safety, purchasing insurance, and controlling financial recovery from losses generated by hazard risk. Enterprise-wide risk management focuses on managing all of the organization's key risks and opportunities with the intent of maximizing the organization's value.

Educational Objective 5

5-1. Elements necessary to describe a loss exposure include the following: (1) an asset exposed to loss, (2) cause of loss (also called a peril), and (3) financial consequences of that loss.

5-2.

a. Property, investments, money that is owed to the organization, cash, intangible assets, and human resources

b. Property, investments, money that is owed to the individual, cash, professional qualifications, a unique skill set, and valuable experience

5-3. Insurers typically define hazards according to the following four classifications: (1) Moral hazard—a condition that increases the frequency and/or severity of loss resulting from a person acting dishonestly, such as exaggerating a loss; (2) morale hazard—a condition that increases the frequency and/or severity of loss resulting from careless or indifferent behavior, such as failing to lock a vehicle; (3) physical hazard—a condition of property, persons, or operations that increases the frequency and/or severity of loss, such as an icy sidewalk; (4) legal hazard—a condition of the legal environment that increases the frequency or severity of loss, such as the fact that courts in certain districts are more likely to award large liability settlements.

5-4. Three factors that affect the financial consequences of a loss include the type of loss exposure, the cause of loss, and the loss frequency and severity.

5-5.

a. Property that has a physical form, such as a piece of equipment

b. Property that has no physical form, such as a patent or copyright

c. Tangible property consisting of land, all structures permanently attached to the land, and whatever is growing on the land

d. All tangible property other than real property

5-6.

a. A loss can result from damage (including destruction, taking, or loss of use) to property in which the person or organization has a financial interest.

b. A loss can result from a claim alleging that the person or organization is legally responsible for bodily injury and/or property damage.

c. A loss can result from a key person's death, disability, retirement, or resignation that deprives an organization of that person's special skill or knowledge.

d. A loss can result from a reduction in net income, often the result of property, liability, or personnel loss.

5-7.

a. ABC's employees may intentionally cause a loss or exaggerate a loss that has occurred, thinking that insurance will pay for it.

b. ABC's employees might drive carelessly, fail to lock an unattended building, or fail to clear an icy sidewalk to protect pedestrians.

c. ABC's employees might increase the likelihood of an accident by failing to correct defects in used cars, putting an excessive number of cars on the lot, or reducing the lighting on the lot.

d. People living in ABC's geographic area might be more litigious than those in other areas, or the local courts might be considered more likely to deliver adverse verdicts or to grant large damage awards in liability suits than those in other areas.

Educational Objective 6

6-1. An organization with an effective risk management program should experience smaller expected losses (less frequent or less severe) and experience less residual uncertainty than a comparable organization that does not practice good risk management. For example, an organization that installs a state-of-the-art security system would expect to have fewer thefts (and therefore lower expected losses) and a better sense of security (less residual uncertainty).

6-2. The overall financial consequence of risk for a given asset or activity is broken down into the following costs:

- Cost of losses not reimbursed by insurance or other external sources
- Cost of insurance premiums
- Cost of external sources of funds, such as interest payments to lenders or transaction costs associated with noninsurance indemnity
- Cost of measures to prevent or reduce the size of potential losses
- Cost of implementing and administering risk management

6-3.

a. Preserves financial resources by reducing an individual's expected losses, and reduces anxiety

b. Preserves financial resources, provides a sense of confidence that capital is protected against future costs, and reduces the deterrence effect of risk

c. Lowers expected losses and improves allocation of productive resources

Educational Objective 7

7-1. Four pre-loss operational goals supported by an effective and efficient risk management program are as follows:

a. Economy of operations—The organization should not incur substantial costs in exchange for slight benefits.

b. Tolerable uncertainty—Keeping manager uncertainty about losses at a tolerable level and providing assurances that losses will be within the bounds of what was anticipated.

c. Legality—Satisfying the organization's legal obligations.

d. Social responsibility—Acting ethically and fulfilling obligations to the community and society as a whole.

7-2. Possible post-loss goals after a significant foreseeable loss has occurred include the following six:

a. Survival

b. Continuity of operations

c. Profitability

d. Earnings stability

e. Social responsibility

f. Growth

7-3. Steps an organization might take to forestall an intolerable shutdown and ensure continuous operations after a loss include the following:

- Identify activities whose interruptions cannot be tolerated
- Identify the types of events that could interrupt such activities
- Determine the standby resources that must be immediately available to counter the effect of those losses
- Ensure the availability of the standby resources at even the most unlikely and difficult times

7-4.

a. Tolerable uncertainty might conflict with the goal of economy of operations because the cost of risk management efforts necessary to reduce uncertainty to a tolerable level may be excessive.

b. Legality might conflict with the goal of economy of operations because some required safety standards could require substantial expense to implement.

c. Social responsibility might conflict with the goal of economy of operations because obligations such as charitable contributions may be expensive.

▶▶

Educational Objective 8

8-1. The six steps in the risk management process are:

a. Identifying loss exposures

b. Analyzing loss exposures

c. Examining feasibility of risk management techniques

d. Selecting the appropriate risk management techniques

e. Implementing selected risk management techniques

f. Monitoring results and revising the risk management program

8-2. Four dimensions used to analyze a loss exposure are as follows:

a. Loss frequency—number of losses within a specific period

b. Loss severity—amount, in dollars, of a loss for a specific occurrence

c. Total dollar losses—total dollar amount of losses for all occurrences in a specified period

d. Timing—when losses occur and when loss payments are made

8-3. Risk control techniques are used to reduce the frequency and severity of loss or make losses more predictable. Risk financing techniques generate funds to finance losses that risk control techniques cannot entirely prevent or reduce.

8-4. An organization might use the following forecasts to analyze the costs of a risk management technique:

- A forecast of the dimensions of expected losses
- A forecast, for each feasible combination of risk management techniques, of the effect on the frequency, severity, and timing of these expected losses
- A forecast of the after-tax costs involved in applying various risk management techniques

8-5. The four steps required to monitor and revise a risk management program are as follows:

a. Establishing standards of acceptable performance

b. Comparing actual results with these standards

c. Correcting substandard performance or revising standards that prove to be unrealistic

d. Evaluating standards that have been substantially exceeded

8-6.

a. Performance standard: Fewer than 1 percent of all customers file claims for damaged shipments.

b. Activities standard: Hourly inspections of floors for spills or other slippery conditions, use of "Caution: wet floor" signs during wet weather conditions.

c. Performance standard: Injury frequency rate reduced by 10 percent from previous year.

Direct Your Learning

ASSIGNMENT 2

Risk Assessment

Educational Objectives

After learning the content of this assignment, you should be able to:

1. Describe the following methods of loss exposure identification:
   - Document analysis
   - Compliance review
   - Personal inspections
   - Expertise within and beyond the organization
2. Explain why data used in risk management decisions need to be relevant, complete, consistent, and organized.
3. Describe the nature of probability with respect to theoretical and empirical probability and the law of large numbers.
4. Explain how the information provided in a simple probability distribution can be used in making basic risk management decisions.
5. Describe the various measures of central tendency and how they can be used in analyzing the probabilities associated with risk.
6. Describe the measures of dispersion and how they can be used in analyzing the probabilities associated with risk.
7. Describe the characteristics of normal distributions and how they can be used to analyze loss exposures and project future losses more accurately.
8. Explain how to analyze loss exposures considering the four dimensions of loss and data credibility.

Outline

- **Identifying Loss Exposures**
  - A. Document Analysis
    1. Risk Assessment Questionnaires and Checklists
    2. Financial Statements and Underlying Accounting Records
    3. Contracts
    4. Insurance Policies
    5. Organizational Policies and Records
    6. Flowcharts and Organizational Charts
    7. Loss Histories
  - B. Compliance Review
  - C. Personal Inspections
  - D. Expertise Within and Beyond the Organization
- **Data Requirements for Exposure Analysis**
  - A. Relevant Data
  - B. Complete Data
  - C. Consistent Data
  - D. Organized Data
- **Nature of Probability**
  - A. Theoretical Probability and Empirical Probability
    1. Law of Large Numbers
- **Using Probability Distributions**
  - A. Outcomes of a Properly Constructed Probability Distribution
    1. Theoretical Probability Distributions
    2. Empirical Probability Distributions
  - B. Discrete and Continuous Probability Distributions
- **Using Central Tendency**
  - A. Expected Value
  - B. Mean
  - C. Median and Cumulative Probabilities
  - D. Mode
- **Using Dispersion**
  - A. Standard Deviation
  - B. Coefficient of Variation
- **Using Normal Distributions**
  - A. Characteristics of Normal Distributions
  - B. Practical Application
- **Analyzing Loss Exposures**
  - A. Loss Frequency
  - B. Loss Severity
    1. Maximum Possible Loss
    2. Frequency and Severity Considered Jointly
  - C. Total Dollar Losses
  - D. Timing
  - E. Data Credibility

s.m.a.r.t. tips

Reduce the number of Key Words and Phrases that you must review. SMART Flash Cards contain the Key Words and Phrases and their definitions, allowing you to set aside those cards that you have mastered.

For each assignment, you should define or describe each of the Key Words and Phrases and answer each of the Review and Application Questions.

Educational Objective 1

Describe the following methods of loss exposure identification:

- **Document analysis**
- **Compliance review**
- **Personal inspections**
- **Expertise within and beyond the organization**

Key Words and Phrases

Balance sheet

Income statement

Statement of cash flows

Hold-harmless agreement (or indemnity agreement)

Indemnification

Hazard analysis

Review Questions

1-1. Identify the types of internal and external documents an organization may use to analyze loss exposures.

1-2. Describe advantages and disadvantages of using questionnaires in assessing loss exposures.

1-3. Describe how an organization uses the following documents to identify loss exposures.

a. Financial statements

b. Contracts

c. Insurance policies

d. Organizational policies and records

e. Flowcharts and organizational charts

f. Loss histories

1-4. Describe how a compliance review may facilitate the identification of loss exposures.

Educational Objective 2

Explain why data used in risk management decisions need to be relevant, complete, consistent, and organized.

Review Questions

2-1. Identify relevant data an organization may use to assess the following types of loss exposures:

a. Property losses

b. Liability losses

c. Personnel losses

d. Net income losses

▶▶

2-2. Describe how complete data can aid a risk management professional in loss exposure assessment.

2-3. Identify two factors in past loss data that must be consistent to avoid underestimating or overestimating loss projections.

Application Question

2-4. The risk management professional of ABC Manufacturing has the following data for losses that have occurred during 2009:

Date	Loss Amount	Cause
1/6/09	$ 500.00	Customer slip and fall
3/17/09	$ 3,500.00	Damage to sales rep auto
3/17/09	$ 800.00	Sales rep injury in auto accident
5/21/09	$ 7,000.00	Assembly line worker back injury
8/11/09	$ 500.00	Office worker back injury

a. If the risk management professional for ABC Manufacturing were trying to analyze employee injuries for workers compensation purposes, what data are relevant?

Data From employees being injured (exclude Companies)

b. Are the data provided complete?

No, need # of people

c. Are the data consistent?

Yes, all in the same year

→ smallest → Largest

d. Organize the employee injury data into an array.

1. office worker - $500
2. Sales Rep - $800
3. Assembly Line Worker - $7,000

Educational Objective 3

Describe the nature of probability with respect to theoretical and empirical probability and the law of large numbers.

Key Words and Phrases

Theoretical probability - Probability that is based on theoretical principles rather than on actual experiences.

Empirical probability (a posteriori probability) - A probability measure that is based on actual experience through historical data or from observation of facts.

Probability analysis - A technique for forecasting events, such as accidental and business losses, on the assumption that they are governed by an unchanging probability distribution.

▶▶

Law of large numbers - A mathematical principle stating that as the number of similar but independent exposures units increases, the relative accuracy of predictions about the future outcomes (losses) also increases.

Review Questions

3-1. Explain the difference between theoretical and empirical probabilities.

Theoretical probability is based on theoretical principles

Empirical probability is based on Actual experiences through historical data or from observation of facts.

3-2. Identify two conditions in which probability analysis is effective for projecting losses.

~~Mutually exclusive + collectively exhaustive~~

(1) A substantial volume of data on past losses

(2) Fairly stable operations so that (except for price level changes) patterns of past losses presumably will continue in the future

3-3. List three criteria necessary to accurately forecast future events based on the law of large numbers.

(1) The events have occurred in the past under substantially ~~[illegible]~~ identical conditions and have resulted from unchanging, basic casual forces.

(2) The events can be expected to occur in the future under the same, unchanging conditions.

(3) The events have been, and will continue to be, both independent of one another and sufficiently numerous.

Educational Objective 4

Explain how the information provided in a simple probability distribution can be used in making basic risk management decisions.

Key Word or Phrase

Probability distribution - A presentation (table, chart or graph) of probability estimates of a particular set of circumstances and of the probability of each possible outcome.

Review Questions

4-1. Identify outcome characteristics common to both theoretical and empirical possibility distributions.

① mutually exclusive
② collectively exhaustive
} The outcomes are both

4-2. List two requirements to construct an empirical probability distribution.

① To provide a mutually exclusive, collectively exhaustive list of outcomes, loss categories (bins) must be designated so that all losses can be included.

② The distribution must define the set of probabilities associated with each of the possible outcomes

4-3. Describe the following two forms of probability distributions and how they are used in analyzing future losses.

a. Discrete probability distributions

Discrete probabilities have finite number of possible outcomes and are typically used to analyze how often something will occur (frequency)

b. Continuous probability distribution

Continuous probability have an infinite number of possible outcomes and are typically used for severity distributions

Application Question

4-4. Construct an empirical probability distribution from the following array of workers compensation losses.

▶▶

Rank	Date	Adjusted Loss Amount
10	12/5	$100
9	08/7	$500
8	01/6	$750
7	02/3	$800
6	02/5	$1,100
5	02/5	$1,500
4	11/8	$1,800
3	07/5	$2,100
2	09/18	$2,800
1	09/4	$10,000

Educational Objective 5

Describe the various measures of central tendency and how they can be used in analyzing the probabilities associated with risk.

Key Words and Phrases

Central tendency

Expected value

Mean

Median

Mode

Review Questions

5-1. Describe mean, median, and mode and how a risk management professional uses them in assessing loss exposures.

5-2. Explain how calculating the expected value is similar to calculating the mean.

The mean is calculated by weighting each observed outcome by the relative frequency with which it occurs. The expected value is calculated by weighting each possible outcome by its probability.

5-3. Explain what knowing the mode of a distribution allows insurance and risk management professionals to do.

Insurance and risk management can focus on the outcomes that are most common

(ie. decisions regarding deductibles when the most common Auto PD losses are known)

▶▶

Application Question

5-4. The underwriter at Millwright Insurance must choose between two accounts to provide insurance coverage. Both accounts have provided a probability distribution based on past losses. Account A's distribution has a mean of $8,500. Account B's distribution has a mean of $10,000. Which account has higher expected losses?

Educational Objective 6

Describe the measures of dispersion and how they can be used in analyzing the probabilities associated with risk.

Key Words and Phrases

Dispersion

Standard deviation

Coefficient of variation

Review Questions

6-1. Describe standard deviation and how insurance and risk management professionals use it in assessing loss exposures.

6-2. Describe coefficient of variation and how insurance and risk management professionals use it in assessing loss exposures.

6-3. Describe the steps used for calculating the standard deviation of a set of individual outcomes not involving probabilities.

6-4. Explain what insurance and risk management professionals can use the coefficient of variation for when evaluating a particular loss control measure.

Application Question

6-5. The underwriter at Millwright Insurance must choose between two accounts to provide insurance coverage. Both accounts have provided a probability distribution based on past losses. Account A's distribution has a mean of $8,500 and a standard deviation of $17,000. Account B's distribution has a mean of $10,000 and a standard deviation of $18,000. Which account has greater variability relative to its mean?

Educational Objective 7

Describe the characteristics of normal distributions and how they can be used to analyze loss exposures and project future losses more accurately.

Key Word or Phrase

Normal distribution

Review Questions

7-1. Describe a normal distribution and why it is useful to a risk management professional in forecasting loss exposures.

7-2. In a normal distribution, what percentage of outcomes is within two standard deviations above or below the mean?

7-3. Describe how the expected value and the standard deviation of a normal distribution can be helpful in making risk management decisions.

Application Question

7-4. Assume that ABC Manufacturing's total losses per year are normally distributed. The average (mean) of the firm's losses is $500,000, and the standard deviation is $40,000. Assuming underlying conditions do not change, what is the probability that its losses next year will be between $460,000 and $540,000? What is the probability that its losses next year will be between $500,000 and $540,000? = 68.26%

* Normally distributed = percentages from 2.39 Book example

(ie. 2.15, 13.59, 34.13 | 34.13, 13.59, 2.15)

Educational Objective 8

Explain how to analyze loss exposures considering the four dimensions of loss and data credibility.

Review Questions

8-1. List four dimensions used in the analysis of a loss exposure.

8-2. List the four categories of loss frequency and the three categories of loss severity used in the Prouty Approach.

8-3. List the three categories of loss severity used in the Prouty Approach.

8-4. Describe two approaches a risk management professional may use when jointly analyzing the frequency and loss severity of a loss exposure.

8-5. Explain why timing is an important consideration when analyzing loss exposures.

8-6. Describe the dilemma that insurance and risk management professionals can have when evaluating data credibility.

▶▶

Answers to Assignment 2 Questions

NOTE: These answers are provided to give students a basic understanding of acceptable types of responses. They often are not the only valid answers and are not intended to provide an exhaustive response to the questions.

Educational Objective 1

1-1. An organization may use the following types of internal and external documents to analyze loss exposures:

- Internal documents—financial statements, accounting records, contracts, insurance policies, policy and procedure manuals, flowcharts and organizational charts, and loss histories
- External documents—questionnaires, checklists, surveys, Web sites, news releases, and reports from external organizations

1-2. The advantage of questionnaires in assessing loss exposures is that they capture more descriptive information than checklists about amounts or values exposed to loss. Their disadvantage is that they typically require considerable expense, time, and effort to complete and may still not identify all loss exposures.

1-3.

a. Balance sheets, income statements, statement of cash flows, and supporting statements help identify major categories of current and past loss exposures and can be used to identify future plans that could lead to new loss exposures. For example, asset entries on a balance sheet indicate property values that could by reduced by loss.

b. Contracts can help identify property and liability loss exposures assumed or transferred by contract and help determine who has assumed responsibility for which loss exposure.

c. Insurance policies can reveal many of the organization's insurable loss exposures.

d. Corporate by-laws, board minutes, employee manuals, procedure manuals, mission statements, and risk management policies may identify existing loss exposures and indicate impending changes that may create new loss exposures.

e. Flowcharts show the nature and use of resources involved in an organization's operations and the sequence of and relationships between the operations. They may also reveal bottlenecks where losses could have substantial effects on business operations. An organizational chart helps identify key personnel for whom the organization may have a personnel loss exposure.

f. An organization's loss history, or that of a comparable organization, can indicate current or future loss exposures.

1-4. Compliance review determines an organization's compliance with local, state, and federal statutes and regulations and can therefore help the organization minimize or avoid liability loss exposures associated with noncompliance.

Educational Objective 2

2-1.

a. Data should include the property's repair or replacement cost at the time it is to be restored.

b. Data should relate to past claims that are substantially the same as the potential future claims being assessed.

c. Data must relate to personnel with similar experience and expertise as those being considered as future loss exposures.

d. Data should involve similar reductions in revenue and similar additional expenses to those of the loss exposures under consideration.

2-2. Having complete data aids in loss exposure assessment by helping isolate the causes of each loss and enabling the risk management professional to make reasonably reliable estimates of the dollar amounts of the future losses.

2-3. These are two factors regarding historical loss data that must be consistent to avoid underestimating or overestimating loss projections:

a. Data must be collected on a consistent basis (same accounting methods) for all recorded losses.

b. Data must be expressed in constant dollars.

2-4.

a. The relevant data are the 3/17 sales rep injury, the 5/21 assembly line worker injury, and the 8/11 office worker injury.

b. The data are not complete; they do not list the specific cause, time of loss, or treatments used.

c. Because all the data are 2009 data, they are consistent.

d. (1) 8/11/09, $500.00; (2) 3/17/09, $800.00; (3) 5/21/09, $7,000.00.

Educational Objective 3

3-1. Theoretical probabilities, based on theoretical principles, are constant as long as the physical conditions that generate them remain unchanged. Empirical probabilities, based on actual experience (historical data), are estimates whose accuracy depends on the size and representative nature of the samples being studied.

3-2. Probability analysis is effective for projecting losses in organizations that have a substantial volume of data on past losses and that have fairly stable operations.

3-3. For accurate forecasts of future events based on the law of large numbers, events must include the following three criteria:

- They must have occurred in the past under substantially identical conditions and have resulted from unchanging, basic causal forces.
- They can be expected to occur in the future under the same, unchanging conditions.
- They have been, and will continue to be, both independent of one another and sufficiently numerous.

Educational Objective 4

4-1. Characteristics common to outcomes of both theoretical and empirical probabilities are that the outcomes are mutually exclusive and collectively exhaustive.

4-2. The following are two requirements to construct an empirical probability distribution:

a. To provide a mutually exclusive, collectively exhaustive list of outcomes, loss categories (bins) must be designated so that all losses can be included.

b. The distribution must define the set of probabilities associated with each of the possible outcomes.

4-3. Discrete probability distributions and continuous probability distributions can be described as follows:

a. Discrete probability distributions have a finite number of possible outcomes and are typically used to analyze how often something will occur (frequency).

b. Continuous probability distributions have an infinite number of possible outcomes and are typically used for severity distributions.

4-4. There are a number of ways to display a probability distribution. One way is to create a table using bins. This example uses $1,000 bin sizes, but other bin sizes are acceptable.

Bin Size	# of Losses	Percentage of Number of Losses
$0–$1,000	4	40%
$1,001–$2000	3	30%
$2,001–$3,000	2	20%
$3,000 +	1	10%
		100%

Educational Objective 5

5-1. Three common measures of central tendency are as follows:

- Mean is the numeric average (the sum of the values in a data set divided by the number of values), often used by a risk management professional as the single best guess to forecast future events.
- Median is the value at the midpoint of a sequential data set with an odd number of values, or the mean of the two middle values. A risk management professional might use the median in selecting retention levels or in selecting upper limits of insurance coverage.
- Mode is the most frequently occurring value in a distribution. It enables risk management professionals to focus on the outcomes that are the most common.

5-2. Just as the expected value is calculated by weighting each possible outcome by its probability, the mean is calculated by weighting each observed outcome by the relative frequency with which it occurs.

5-3. Knowing the mode of a distribution allows insurance and risk management professionals to focus on the outcomes that are the most common. For example, knowing that the most common auto physical damage losses are in the $0–$10,000 range may influence the risk financing decisions regarding deductible levels for potential insurance coverages.

5-4. The underwriter's decision regarding Millwright Insurance accounts A and B considers, among other things, the expected losses of each account, which are higher for Account B because the mean of past losses for it is $10,000 and only $8,500 for A.

Educational Objective 6

6-1. Standard deviation indicates how widely dispersed the values in a distribution are. It provides a measure of how sure an insurance or risk management professional can be in projecting the frequency or severity of losses.

6-2. Coefficient of variation is used to compare two distributions with different means. It could help an underwriter determine to which account to offer coverage or help a risk management professional determine whether a particular loss control measure has made losses more or less predictable.

6-3. The steps for calculating the standard deviation of a set of individual outcomes not involving probabilities are these:

- Calculate the mean of the outcomes (the sum of the outcomes divided by the number of outcomes)
- Subtract the mean from each of the outcomes
- Square each of the resulting differences
- Sum these squares
- Divide this sum by the number of outcomes minus one (this value is called the variance)
- Calculate the square root of the variance

6-4. Insurance and risk management professionals can use the coefficient of variation to determine whether a particular loss control measure has made losses more or less predictable (that is, whether the distribution is more or less variable).

6-5. The coefficient of variation is used to determine which account has greater variability relative to its mean.

$$A = \frac{17,000}{8,500} = 2$$

$$B = \frac{18,000}{10,000} = 1.8$$

Therefore, A has greater variability.

Educational Objective 7

7-1. A normal distribution is a probability distribution that, when graphed, generates a bell-shaped curve. It is useful to a risk management professional in accurately forecasting the variability around the mean of many physical phenomena.

7-2. In a normal distribution, 95.44 percent of outcomes are within two standard deviations above or below the mean.

7-3. The characteristics of the expected value and standard deviation of a normal distribution can help management select an acceptable probability for loss and aid in scheduling maintenance or selecting retention levels on various loss exposures.

7-4. The probability that ABC Manufacturing's loss probability would be between $460,000 and $540,000 is 68.26 percent. The probability that ABC Manufacturing's loss probability would be between $500,000 and $540,000 is 34.13 percent.

Educational Objective 8

8-1. These are the four dimensions used in the analysis of a loss exposure:

- Loss frequency—number of losses that occur within a specific period
- Loss severity—dollar amount of loss for a specific occurrence
- Total dollar losses—total dollar amount of losses for all occurrences during a specific period
- Timing—when losses occur and when loss payments are made

8-2. These are the four categories of loss frequency used in the Prouty Approach:

- Almost nil
- Slight
- Moderate
- Definite

▸▸

8-3. These are the three categories of loss severity used in the Prouty Approach:

- Slight
- Significant
- Severe

8-4. Risk management professionals may use two approaches when jointly analyzing the frequency and loss severity of a loss exposure:

- Prouty Approach—identifies four categories of loss frequency and three categories of loss severity
- Total claims distribution—created by combining the frequency and severity distributions

8-5. Timing is important to consider when analyzing loss exposures because of the time value of money. Money held in reserve can earn interest until the payment is made. In addition, when a loss is counted affects accounting and tax treatment.

8-6. Insurance and risk management professionals can be left with a dilemma answering whether it is better to use older data, which are accurate but may have been generated in an environment that is substantially different from the that of the period for which they are trying to predict, or to use more recent data and sacrifice some accuracy to maintain the integrity of the environment.

Direct Your Learning

ASSIGNMENT 3

Risk Control

Educational Objectives

After learning the content of this assignment, you should be able to:

1. Describe the six categories of risk control techniques in terms of the following:
   - Whether each reduces loss frequency, reduces loss severity, or makes losses more predictable
   - How each can be used to address a particular loss exposure
   - How they differ from one another
2. Explain how an organization can use risk control techniques and measures to achieve the following risk control goals:
   - Implement effective and efficient risk control measures
   - Comply with legal requirements
   - Promote life safety
   - Ensure business continuity
3. Explain how risk control techniques can be applied to property, liability, personnel, and net income loss exposures.
4. Describe business continuity management in terms of its scope, the process used to implement it, and the contents of a typical business continuity plan.

Outline

- **Risk Control Techniques**
  - A. Avoidance
  - B. Loss Prevention
  - C. Loss Reduction
  - D. Separation
  - E. Duplication
  - F. Diversification
- **Risk Control Goals**
  - A. Implement Effective and Efficient Risk Control Measures
  - B. Comply With Legal Requirements
  - C. Promote Life Safety
  - D. Ensure Business Continuity
- **Application of Risk Control Techniques**
  - A. Property Loss Exposures
  - B. Liability Loss Exposures
  - C. Personnel Loss Exposures
  - D. Net Income Loss Exposures
- **Business Continuity Management**
  - A. Scope of Business Continuity Management
  - B. Business Continuity Process
  - C. Business Continuity Plan

s.m.a.r.t. tips

Actively capture information by using the open space in the SMART Review Notes to write out key concepts. Putting information into your own words is an effective way to push that information into your memory.

For each assignment, you should define or describe each of the Key Words and Phrases and answer each of the Review and Application Questions.

Educational Objective 1

Describe the six categories of risk control techniques in terms of the following:

- **Whether each reduces loss frequency, reduces loss severity, or makes losses more predictable**
- **How each can be used to address a particular loss exposure**
- **How they differ from one another**

Key Words and Phrases

Risk control

Avoidance

Loss prevention

Loss reduction

Disaster recovery plan

Separation

Duplication

Diversification

Review Questions

1-1. Explain how proactive and reactive avoidance differ in reducing loss frequency of a loss exposure.

1-2. Describe the purpose of the following loss reduction measures in controlling losses.

a. Pre-loss measures

b. Post-loss measures

1-3. Describe the purpose of a disaster recovery plan.

1-4. Identify circumstances in which each of the following techniques would be an effective choice for loss reduction.

a. Separation

b. Duplication

c. Diversification

Educational Objective 2

Explain how an organization can use risk control techniques and measures to achieve the following risk control goals:

- **Implement effective and efficient risk control measures**
- **Comply with legal requirements**
- **Promote life safety**
- **Ensure business continuity**

Key Word or Phrase

Life safety

Review Questions

2-1. Describe the advantages of using cash flow analysis for the selection of risk control measures.

2-2. Describe the disadvantages of using cash flow analysis for the selection of risk control measures.

2-3. List the types of state or federal statutes an organization may need to consider when selecting risk control measures in order to comply with legal requirements.

2-4. Identify possible consequences an organization can face for failure to comply with legal requirements.

2-5. Identify the issues regarding fire, health, and safety a risk management professional should consider when assessing an organization's life-safety loss exposures.

2-6. Identify causes of loss an organization should consider when promoting life safety.

Educational Objective 3

Explain how risk control techniques can be applied to property, liability, personnel, and net income loss exposures.

Review Questions

3-1. Identify the factors insurance producers and underwriters commonly consider when examining loss exposures in commercial properties.

3-2. Which risk control techniques are commonly used to control liability loss exposures?

3-3. Describe loss prevention and loss reduction measures an organization might use to control work-related injury and illness.

Application Question

3-4. The Cooper Pharmaceutical Company manufactures and distributes both prescription drugs and medicines sold over the counter by pharmacies and other outlets. More than half of Cooper's annual expenses are for research and development of new products. About 50 percent of Cooper's revenues are derived from an ulcer remedy. The remedy's formula includes a chemical compound that is manufactured in only one chemical plant in the world. There are other similar ulcer remedies on the market, and management concedes that some of them are equally effective. However, Cooper's product was the first on the market and has acquired a large following among doctors, who usually prescribe it by Cooper's brand name. Management is concerned that any prolonged absence of their ulcer medicine from the market would cause doctors to prescribe another brand, and they might not return to Cooper's brand when it becomes available again.

The testing process for some products is long and complex, sometimes involving several years of testing on dogs, primates, or other relatively long-lived animals, possibly followed by testing on human volunteers. Voluminous records accumulate during such tests and must be retained for many years for use in licensing applications, defense of products liability claims, and future research projects.

▶▶

Cooper stores its research records in fire-resistive filing cabinets in the records room of its research center. The center also houses research laboratories, offices for research personnel, and animals for research. The research center is located in a sprinklered, fire-resistive building adjacent to Cooper's factory. Personnel who handle the animals are thoroughly trained in animal care to ensure the safety of both the animals and employees. Although Cooper has more than 200 employees, its workers compensation claims have been well below the industry average over the last ten years.

The factory building also is fire resistive and is sprinklered in all areas except the clean room. The clean room, used for manufacturing and packaging processes that require complete sterility, has its own air conditioning system with special filtering equipment to eliminate dust and other potential contaminants and other equipment to maintain the sterile atmosphere. Even very slight contamination of the clean room would require the discontinuation of production for several days until sterility could be reestablished. All workers in the clean room must wear special sterile uniforms and surgical masks.

Identify the risk control measures used by Cooper for each of the following loss exposures.

a. Property loss exposures

b. Personnel loss exposures

c. Net income loss exposures

Educational Objective 4

Describe business continuity management in terms of its scope, the process used to implement it, and the contents of a typical business continuity plan.

Review Questions

4-1. Explain the purpose of business continuity management.

4-2. Identify potential situations that business continuity management might address to help achieve an organization's goal of survival and continuity of operations after a loss.

4-3. List the six steps in the business continuity process.

4-4. Identify guidelines for design of an effective business continuity plan.

4-5. List the content commonly contained in business continuity plans.

Answers to Assignment 3 Questions

NOTE: These answers are provided to give students a basic understanding of acceptable types of responses. They often are not the only valid answers and are not intended to provide an exhaustive response to the questions.

Educational Objective 1

1-1. Proactive avoidance seeks to avoid a loss exposure before it exists, such as by choosing not to engage in an activity. Reactive avoidance seeks to eliminate a loss exposure that already exists, such as by discontinuing an existing activity. Both avoidance methods avoid loss exposures from future activities. Reactive avoidance does not eliminate loss exposures from past activities.

1-2. These loss reduction measures control losses in the following ways:

a. Pre-loss measures are applied before a loss occurs. They reduce the amount or extent of property damaged and the number of people injured or the extent of injury incurred from a single event.

b. Post-loss measures are applied after a loss occurs. They focus on emergency procedures, salvage operations, rehabilitation activities, public relations, or legal defenses to halt the spread or to counter the effects of a loss.

1-3. The purpose of a disaster recovery plan is to ensure that critical resources are available to facilitate an organization's continuity of operations in an emergency. The plan typically includes backup procedures, emergency response, and post-disaster recovery.

1-4. The techniques listed would be effective choices for loss reduction in the following situations:

a. Separation is appropriate if the organization can operate with only a portion of the separated assets or locations left intact.

b. Duplication is appropriate if an entire asset or activity is so important that the consequence of its loss justifies the expense and time of maintaining a duplicate.

c. Diversification is more commonly applied to business risks than to hazard risks. Organizations engage in diversification by providing a variety of products and services that are used by a range of customers.

Educational Objective 2

2-1. An organization's use of cash flow analysis in its selection of risk control measures offers the following advantages:

- Helps achieve the organization's value-maximization goal by providing a basis of comparison for all value-maximizing decisions.
- Increases efficiency by reducing unnecessary expenditures on risk control.

2-2. Disadvantages of using cash flow analysis for selection of risk control measures include the following:

- Weakness of the assumptions that often must be made to conduct the analysis
- Difficulty of accurately estimating future cash flows
- Lack of consideration of nonfinancial goals or selection criteria

2-3. To comply with legal requirements when selecting risk control measures, an organization should consider state or federal statutes regarding fire safety codes, environmental regulations, workers compensation laws, and disability laws.

2-4. An organization can face fines, sanctions, or liability for failure to comply with legal requirements.

2-5. When assessing an organization's fire, health, and safety loss exposures, a risk management professional should consider the characteristics of the people who occupy the building and the types of building occupancies.

2-6. When promoting life safety, an organization should consider causes of loss such as fire safety, product safety, building collapse, industrial accidents, environmental pollution, and exposure to hazardous activities that may create the possibility of injury or death.

Educational Objective 3

3-1. When examining loss exposures in commercial properties, insurance producers and underwriters consider construction, occupancy, protection, and environment (COPE).

3-2. Three risk control techniques are commonly used to control liability losses: avoidance of the activity, loss prevention, and loss reduction.

3-3. An organization may control work-related injury and illness through loss prevention by using education, training, and safety measures.

Loss reduction measures for work-related injury and illness include emergency response training and rehabilitation management.

3-4. The risk control measures Cooper is currently using include the following:

a. For property loss exposures—using fire-resistive construction and sprinklers.

b. For personnel loss exposures—thorough training of staff handling animals.

c. For net income loss exposures—in addition to the risk control measures just mentioned, Cooper's diversification of product offerings through research and development of new products reduces the net income exposure related to the ulcer remedy.

Educational Objective 4

4-1. The purpose of business continuity management is to identify potential threats to an organization and to provide a methodology for ensuring the organization's continued business operations. Business continuity management is designed to meet the organizational post-loss goals of survival and continuity of operations.

4-2. Business continuity management can address the following potential situations in order to help achieve an organization's goal of survival and continuity of operations after a loss: interruptions from property losses, information technology (IT) problems, human failures (such as fraud), loss of utility services or infrastructure, reputation losses, and human asset (personnel) losses.

4-3. The following are the six steps in the business continuity process:

a. Identify the organization's critical functions

b. Identify the risks (threats) to the organization's critical functions

c. Evaluate the effect of the risks on those critical functions

d. Develop a business continuity strategy

e. Develop a business continuity plan

f. Monitor and revise the business continuity process

4-4. Guidelines for design of an effective business continuity plan include the following:

- Design a clear plan that can be quickly read and understood
- Provide copies of the plan to all relevant parties
- Provide appropriate training, including periodic rehearsals of crisis procedures

4-5. Business continuity plans commonly contain the following content:

- Strategy the organization will follow to manage the crisis
- Information about the roles and duties of various individuals in the organization
- Steps that can be taken to prevent any further loss or damage
- Emergency response plan to deal with life and safety issues
- Crisis management plan to deal with communication and reputation issues
- Business recovery and restoration plan to deal with losses to property, processes, or products
- Access to stress management and counseling for affected parties

Direct Your Learning

ASSIGNMENT 4

Risk Financing

Educational Objectives

After learning the content of this assignment, you should be able to:

1. Explain how individuals or organizations can achieve their overall and risk management goals by fulfilling the following risk financing goals:
   - Pay for losses
   - Manage the cost of risk
   - Manage cash flow variability
   - Maintain an appropriate level of liquidity
   - Comply with legal requirements
2. Describe the following aspects of retention and transfer:
   - Retention funding measures
   - Limitations on risk transfer measures
   - The advantages of both retention and transfer
3. Explain how the following can affect the selection of the appropriate risk financing measure:
   - Ability of a risk financing measure to meet risk financing goals
   - Loss exposure characteristics
   - Characteristics specific to an individual or organization
4. Explain how an organization meets its risk financing goals by using the following risk financing measures:
   - Guaranteed cost insurance
   - Self-insurance
   - Large deductible plans
   - Captives

Educational Objectives, continued

- Finite risk plans
- Pools
- Retrospective rating plans
- Hold-harmless agreements
- Capital market solutions

Outline

- **Risk Financing Goals**
  - A. Pay for Losses
  - B. Manage the Cost of Risk
  - C. Manage Cash Flow Variability
  - D. Maintain an Appropriate Level of Liquidity
  - E. Comply With Legal Requirements
- **Retention and Transfer**
  - A. Retention and Transfer in Same Risk Financing Measure
  - B. Retention
    1. Retention Funding Measures
    2. Advantages of Retention
  - C. Transfer
    1. Limitations on Risk Transfer Measures
    2. Advantages of Transfer
- **Selecting Appropriate Risk Financing Measures**
  - A. Mix of Retention and Transfer
  - B. Loss Exposure Characteristics
  - C. Individual- or Organization-Specific Characteristics
    1. Risk Tolerance
    2. Financial Condition
    3. Core Operations
    4. Ability to Diversify
    5. Ability to Control Losses
    6. Ability to Administer the Retention Plan
- **Risk Financing Measures**
  - A. Guaranteed Cost Insurance
  - B. Self-Insurance
  - C. Large Deductible Plans
  - D. Captive Insurers
    1. Operation of a Captive
    2. Special Types of Group Captives
    3. Ability of a Captive to Meet Risk Financing Goals
  - E. Finite Risk Insurance Plans
  - F. Pools
  - G. Retrospective Rating Plans
    1. Design
    2. Loss Exposures
    3. Loss Limit
    4. Minimum and Maximum Premiums
    5. Administration
    6. Cost Savings
    7. Risk Control
    8. Financial Impact
    9. Risk Financing Goals
  - H. Hold-Harmless Agreements
  - I. Capital Market Solutions
    1. Securitization
    2. Hedging
  - J. Contingent Capital Arrangements
    1. Ability of Capital Market Solutions to Meet Risk Financing Goals
    2. Combinations of Risk Financing Measures

Use the SMART Online Practice Exams to test your understanding of the course material. You can review questions over a single assignment or multiple assignments, or you can take an exam over the entire course.

For each assignment, you should define or describe each of the Key Words and Phrases and answer each of the Review and Application Questions.

Educational Objective 1

Explain how individuals or organizations can achieve their overall and risk management goals by fulfilling the following risk financing goals:

- **Pay for losses**
- **Manage the cost of risk**
- **Manage cash flow variability**
- **Maintain an appropriate level of liquidity**
- **Comply with legal requirements**

Review Questions

1-1. Describe the expenses that constitute an organization's cost of risk regardless of whether losses are retained or transferred.

1-2. Identify the factors that affect an organization's maximum cash flow variability level.

1-3. Describe internal and external methods an organization might use to increase cash liquidity.

Educational Objective 2

Describe the following aspects of retention and transfer:

- **Retention funding measures**
- **Limitations on risk transfer measures**
- **The advantages of both retention and transfer**

Key Words and Phrases

Retention

Transfer

Review Questions

2-1. Describe the four planned retention funding techniques available to an organization.

2-2. Identify two limitations on the risk transfer measures available to individuals and organizations.

2-3. Identify the advantages of each of the following risk financing techniques:

a. Retention

b. Transfer

Educational Objective 3

Explain how the following can affect the selection of the appropriate risk financing measure:

- **Ability of a risk financing measure to meet risk financing goals**
- **Loss exposure characteristics**
- **Characteristics specific to an individual or organization**

Review Questions

3-1. Describe the respective abilities of using retention and transfer to meet an organization's risk financing goals.

▶▶

3-2. Identify the loss exposure characteristics that help an organization determine which loss exposures to retain and which to transfer.

3-3. Explain how the following individual- or organization-specific characteristics affect retention levels.

a. Risk tolerance

b. Financial condition

c. Core operations

d. Ability to diversify

e. Ability to control losses

f. Ability to administer the retention plan

Educational Objective 4

Explain how an organization meets its risk financing goals by using the following risk financing measures:

- **Guaranteed cost insurance**
- **Self-insurance**
- **Large deductible plans**
- **Captives**
- **Finite risk plans**
- **Pools**
- **Retrospective rating plans**
- **Hold-harmless agreements**
- **Capital market solutions**

Key Words and Phrases

Primary layer

▶▶

Excess layer

Excess coverage

Umbrella policy

Buffer layer

Self-insurance

Large deductible plan

Captive insurer, or captive

Risk retention group

Rent-a-captive

Protected cell company (PCC)

Finite risk insurance plan

Pool

Retrospective rating plan

Loss limit

Capital market

Securitization

Insurance securitization

Hedging

Derivative

Contingent capital arrangement

▶▶

Review Questions

4-1. Explain the difference between a self-insurance plan and a large deductible plan.

4-2. Identify decisions regarding the following that an organization should consider when establishing a captive:

a. Captive operation

b. Domicile selection

4-3. Describe three special types of group captives.

4-4. Describe how organizations typically benefit from using the following risk financing plans:

a. Pools

b. Retrospective rating plans

4-5. Describe the advantages and disadvantages of using hedging as a risk financing measure.

Answers to Assignment 4 Questions

NOTE: These answers are provided to give students a basic understanding of acceptable types of responses. They often are not the only valid answers and are not intended to provide an exhaustive response to the questions.

Educational Objective 1

1-1. The following expenses constitute an organization's cost of risk regardless of whether losses are retained or transferred:

- Administrative expenses—include the cost of internal administration and the cost of purchased services.
- Risk control expenses—incurred to reduce loss frequency, reduce the severity of losses, or increase the predictability of future losses.
- Risk financing expenses—incurred to manage the risk financing measures used to meet risk financing goals.

1-2. An organization's maximum cash flow variability level depends on the organization's size, its financial strength, management's degree of risk tolerance, and the degree to which the organization's stakeholders are willing to accept risk.

1-3. An organization might use the following methods to increase cash liquidity:

- Internal method—selling assets or retaining cash flow
- External method—borrowing, issuing a debt instrument, or issuing stock

Educational Objective 2

2-1. The four planned retention funding techniques available to an organization are as follows:

- Current expensing of losses—an approach that relies on current cash flows to cover the cost of losses
- Using an unfunded reserve—an accounting entry recognizing the organization's potential liability to pay for a loss, but not specifying the assets that are to pay for a potential loss
- Using a funded reserve—a reserve supported with cash, securities, or other liquid assets allocated to meet the obligations that the reserve represents
- Borrowing funds—an approach that indirectly uses an organization's own resources to pay for losses and in time uses its own earnings to repay the loan

2-2. The following are two limitations on the risk transfer measures available to individuals and organizations:

- Risk transfer measures are not typically pure transfers but are some combination of retention and transfer. The individual or organization pays at least some portion of the loss.
- The ultimate responsibility for paying for the loss remains with the individual or organization. If the other party (such as an insurer) cannot or will not pay for a loss, the loss must be absorbed by the individual or organization.

2-3. The advantages of these risk financing techniques are as follows:

a. Advantages of using retention as a risk financing technique include cost savings, control of the claims process, timing of cash flows, and incentives for risk control.

b. Advantages of using transfer as a risk financing technique include reducing exposure to large losses, reducing cash flow variability, providing ancillary services, and avoiding adverse employee and public relations.

Educational Objective 3

3-1. Using retention to meet risk financing goals can be the most economical risk financing measure, depending on how the organization structures and manages its retention. Using transfer to meet risk financing goals typically offers the organization the greatest certainty regarding its ability to pay losses and the greatest cash flow certainty and is also useful in preventing liquidity problems.

3-2. Frequency and severity are two loss exposure characteristics that help an organization determine which loss exposures to retain and which to transfer. For most loss exposures, risk financing through retention is appropriate. For low-frequency, high-severity loss exposures, risk transfer measures are appropriate.

3-3.

a. Generally, the higher an individual's or organization's willingness to accept risk, the higher the likelihood that more risk will be retained.

b. The more financially secure an individual or organization is, the more loss exposures it can retain without causing liquidity or cash flow variability problems.

c. An organization is better able to retain loss exposures directly related to its core operations.

d. If an organization can diversify its loss exposures, it can offset losses that occur and can more accurately forecast future losses.

e. The more risk control an organization can undertake, the more loss exposures it can typically retain.

f. Organizations that can fulfill the greater administrative requirements of retention (claim administration, risk management consulting, or retention fund accounting) can use retention more efficiently.

Educational Objective 4

4-1. The difference between a self-insurance plan and a large deductible plan is the following:

- Self insurance—The insured is responsible for adjusting and paying its own losses up to the attachment point of the excess coverage insurance.
- Large deductible plan—The insurer adjusts and pays all claims. The insurer then seeks reimbursement from the insured for claims that fall below the deductible level.

4-2. When establishing a captive, an organization should consider the following issues:

a. Types of loss exposures the captive will cover, domicile, and whether business outside the parent's business will be accepted

b. Initial capital requirements, taxes, and annual fees; reputation and regulatory environment; premium and investment restrictions; and support of infrastructure in terms of accountants, bankers, lawyers, captive managers, and other third-party services within the domicile.

4-3. Three special types of group captives are as follows:

- Risk retention group (RRG)—A group captive formed under the requirements of the Liability Risk Retention Act of 1986 to insure parent organizations.
- Rent-a-captive—An arrangement under which an organization rents capital from a captive to which it pays premiums and receives reimbursement for its losses.
- Protected cell company (PCC)—A corporate entity separated into cells so that each participating company owns an entire cell but only a portion of the overall company. Because a statute requires the PCC to be separated into cells, each member is assured that other members and third parties cannot access its assets in the event that any of those other members become insolvent. This protection is not necessarily provided by a rent-a-captive.

4-4. Organizations benefit from using risk financing plans, as follows:

a. Pools can reduce an organization's cost of risk and keep the uncertainty of the cost associated with its retained losses at a tolerable level. They are often used by organizations that are too small to use a captive insurer.

b. Retrospective rating plans can provide financial stability if the loss limit and maximum premium are set at the proper levels. If a retrospective rating plan covers more than one type of loss exposure, the insured benefits from the stability provided through diversification by retaining losses from different types of loss exposures under a single plan.

4-5. Using hedging as a risk financing measure has the following advantages and disadvantages:

- Advantages—Hedging against possible net income losses from price changes can reduce an organization's business risk loss exposures and reduce its dependence on traditional financial and insurance markets for its risk transfer needs.
- Disadvantage—Hedging can destabilize an organization's general risk financing plan and its entire financial structure if earnings or surpluses are seriously jeopardized by speculative investments in hedging instruments.

Direct Your Learning

ASSIGNMENT 5

Enterprise-Wide Risk Management

Educational Objectives

After learning the content of this assignment, you should be able to:

1. Contrast traditional risk management and enterprise-wide risk management (ERM).
2. Explain how an organization can improve its strategic decision making by incorporating enterprise-wide risk management (ERM).
3. Explain why enterprise-wide risk management (ERM) is an effective approach to use to face business uncertainties.
4. Summarize the major risk management frameworks and standards.

Outline

- **Traditional Risk Management Versus ERM**
  - A. Risk Categories
  - B. Strategic Integration
  - C. Performance Metrics
  - D. Organizational Structure
- **Improving Strategic Decision Making With ERM**
  - A. Improving Strategic Decision Making
  - B. Integrating ERM and Strategic Planning
    1. Develop ERM Goals (Establish the Internal and External Contexts)
    2. Analyze, Evaluate, and Prioritize Critical Risks (Risk Assessment)
    3. Treat Critical Risks, Considering Priority (Risk Treatment)
    4. Monitor Critical Risks (Monitor and Review)
  - C. Emerging Legal and Regulatory Requirements Regarding ERM
- **ERM in Approaching Business Uncertainties**
  - A. Enhanced Decision Making
    1. Increased Profitability (Economic Efficiency)
    2. Reduced Volatility
    3. Improved Ability to Meet Strategic Goals
    4. Increased Management Accountability
  - B. Improved Risk Communication
    1. Management Consensus
    2. Stakeholder Acceptance
- **Major Risk Management Frameworks and Standards**
  - A. ISO 31000:2009
  - B. BS 31100
  - C. COSO II
  - D. AS/NZS 4360
  - E. FERMA
  - F. Basel II and Solvency II
  - G. Sub-Frameworks

s.m.a.r.t. tips

The SMART Online Practice Exams product contains a final practice exam. You should take this exam only when you have completed your study of the entire course. It will be your best indicator of how well prepared you are.

For each assignment, you should define or describe each of the Key Words and Phrases and answer each of the Review and Application Questions.

Educational Objective 1

Contrast traditional risk management and enterprise-wide risk management (ERM).

Key Words and Phrases

Pure risk

Speculative risk

Chief risk officer

Review Questions

1-1. Explain the difference between traditional risk management and ERM.

1-2. List the four areas in which traditional risk management differs from ERM.

1-3. Describe two categories of risk (pure risk) associated with traditional risk management.

1-4. Describe two categories of risk specifically associated with ERM.

1-5. Provide an example of an upside risk.

1-6. Explain how ERM's strategic integration varies from traditional risk management.

1-7. Explain how ERM differs from traditional risk management with regard to organizational structure.

1-8. Explain the role of the chief risk officer in an organization's strategic process.

1-9. Explain the iterative and recursive processes of ERM.

Educational Objective 2

Explain how an organization can improve its strategic decision making by incorporating enterprise-wide risk management (ERM).

Key Word or Phrase

Business model

Review Questions

2-1. An organization develops ERM goals as the first step in integrating ERM into its strategic planning. What types of considerations are included in an organization's ERM goals?

2-2. What is the purpose of an organization's board and executive team assessment of risks as they relate to the organization's mission, strategies, and goals?

2-3. Possible treatments for risks to an organization's strategy include some traditional risk management treatments, such as avoidance and transfer. What additional treatments are applied in ERM?

2-4. How do an organization's executives monitor risks to its strategy?

Educational Objective 3

Explain why enterprise-wide risk management (ERM) is an effective approach to use to face business uncertainties.

Review Questions

3-1. Summarize the two important benefits of the ERM approach.

3-2. Explain how an ERM approach increases profitability.

3-3. Explain how an ERM approach can result in reduced earnings volatility for an organization.

3-4. Summarize how an ERM approach improves an organization's ability to meet strategic goals.

3-5. Explain how the ERM process can lead to increased management accountability.

3-6. Summarize how management consensus is achieved in an organization utilizing an ERM approach.

3-7. Describe how an ERM approach will improve an organization's acceptance by internal and external stakeholders.

Educational Objective 4

Summarize the major risk management frameworks and standards.

Review Questions

4-1. Describe the purpose and focus of ISO 31000:2009.

4-2. Excluding ISO 31000:2009, list four frameworks and standards that are recognized as best practices for risk management implementation.

4-3. Differentiate between Basel II and Solvency II.

Answers to Assignment 5 Questions

NOTE: These answers are provided to give students a basic understanding of acceptable types of responses. They often are not the only valid answers and are not intended to provide an exhaustive response to the questions.

Educational Objective 1

1-1. Traditional risk management considers only hazard and operational risks that can affect an organization. ERM expands an organization's risk focus to include financial and strategic risks, allowing it to account for all eventualities that can affect its ability to achieve its goals.

1-2. These are the four areas in which traditional risk management differs from ERM:

- Risk categories
- Strategic integration
- Performance metrics
- Organizational structure

1-3. These are the two categories of risk associated with traditional risk management:

- Hazard risks are pure risks that include damage to property from perils such as fire and explosion or losses stemming from accidents and injuries to employees or customers.
- Operational risks are pure risks that arise out of service, processing, or manufacturing activities.

1-4. These are two categories of risk specifically associated with ERM:

- Financial risks, which include interest rate risk, competitive risk, inflation, and market-timing risks, among others
- Strategic risks, which include management decisions regarding new products, emerging competitors, and planning issues

1-5. An upside risk is the risk that the organization will outperform its strategic goals. Examples of upside risks include situations in which a business venture experiences an unexpected increase in revenue or market share. Such changes can present the organization with both opportunities and threats.

1-6. By linking risk to the entire enterprise, the organization decouples its financial, strategic, operational, hazard, and other risks from individual operational silos and addresses them within strategy as a whole. Thus, ERM considers the global array of risks that affect the organization.

1-7. The traditional risk manager generally reports to an organizational department such as finance, operations, or legal. Quite often, the responsibility for pure risk management may be localized within a risk management department, which then orchestrates the risk management plan as a central authority. Conversely, in ERM, risk management responsibility is decentralized and integrated into all levels of the organization.

1-8. The chief risk officer's responsibility in the strategic process is to help the organization develop tools that identify and manage events and perils that may cause variation from the achievement of specific strategic goals.

1-9. The iterative aspect of ERM is that the risk management process is engaged to identify and manage each discoverable risk. The recursive aspect of ERM is that the risk management process is revisited on a regular basis to maintain its optimization in relationship to strategic goals.

Educational Objective 2

2-1. ERM goals include considerations regarding the organization's risk appetite, why the organization is establishing the ERM program, the business or organizational need for an ERM program, the intended scope of the ERM program, how ERM will assist the organization in meeting its strategic goals, how the organization defines ERM, whether the organization has a function- or department-focused culture or a collaborative culture, and how that will affect ERM implementation.

2-2. An organization's board and executives assess risks to identify threats that can undermine the organization and to identify opportunities that can benefit the organization. These risks involve changes in competition, customers, technology, the economy, politics, and regulation. Each risk to the organization's strategies is examined because it may affect the organization's success and sustainability.

2-3. Additional treatments for risks to strategy include these:

- Accept—Accept the risk by planning for ways to deal with the uncertainty if it occurs.
- Mitigate—Initiate activities to reduce the probability, impact, or timing of a risk event to an acceptable risk tolerance.
- Optimize/exploit—Develop actions to optimize positive consequences to achieve gains.

2-4. Risks to strategy are monitored by trends, triggering events, and warning signs that were identified during the assessment phase for each risk identified. Information will come from a variety of sources, such as newsletters, regulatory announcements, and surveys. For risks that pose potentially high severity and likelihood, an organization may seek relationships with key individuals in positions to know when changes are imminent that can trigger conditions that could result in an event. With such information, the organization can be prepared to launch treatments.

Educational Objective 3

3-1. These are the two important benefits of the ERM approach:

- Enhanced decision making—An ERM approach allows an organization to systematically explore new opportunities for economic efficiencies while managing threats that stem from internal and external contexts.
- Improved risk communication—ERM also encourages an organization to widely communicate its risk management approach across all of its layers. This includes making all managers aware of the need to identify obstacles that could interfere with achievement of the organization's strategic goals.

3-2. An ERM approach monitors systemic risks inherent in the organization that can adversely affect its long-term financial outlook. When an organization adopts an ERM approach, unexpected occurrences or variations cause much less disruption because the organization has already incorporated the possibility of such occurrences or variations into its decision-making process, allowing it to increase its profitability.

3-3. In addition to maintaining cash flows and balancing its budget, an organization must manage its cash flows to ensure an adequate pipeline of capital to meet challenges and to explore strategic growth opportunities. ERM provides a systematic framework that allows organizations to deploy capital through organization-wide decision making, which ultimately results in stable earnings projections to fund future projects.

3-4. An ERM approach improves an organization's ability to meet strategic goals by providing for organization-wide involvement in the strategic formulation and decision-making process. This process examines factors in the internal and external environments to identify risks that would impede growth and achievement of established goals. ERM can minimize variation through thorough risk identification and assessment, thus improving the organization's ability to meet its strategic goals.

3-5. Those closest to a particular risk are in the best position to evaluate and manage it. The board and senior executives establish the organization's overall mission, vision, and strategic goals, but each manager is responsible and accountable for decision making about risks within his or her individual unit. ERM increases management accountability, leading to improved corporate practices and greater managerial understanding of and consensus regarding corporate strategy.

3-6. ERM improves management consensus by creating a corporate culture that embraces risk as an additional component of each decision. By empowering all managers to consider risk optimization and the cost of risk, ERM provides them with complete information about the potential effects of a decision, including its downsides and upsides. This builds a sense of management by consensus, as opposed to the traditional hierarchal model of management, in which a series of decisions is driven from the top down.

3-7. ERM improves acceptance by internal stakeholders by building a spirit of cooperation among management. Managers will build an understanding that the way they manage risk will have a positive impact on the organization, which, in turn, will benefit them personally.

Educational Objective 4

4-1. ISO 31000:2009 is a publication issued by the International Organization for Standardization. ISO 31000:2009 provides an international standard for risk management as well as a generic approach to risk management applicable within any industry sector. It focuses on commonly accepted principles, such as meeting goals and the importance of risk communication. Overall, the standard emphasizes that risk management is integral to an organization's structures, strategies, and goals.

4-2. Four other frameworks and standards are these:

- BS 31100 (British Standard Institution)
- COSO II (Committee of Sponsoring Organizations of the Treadway Commission)
- AS/NZS 4360 (Australian/New Zealand Standard for ERM)
- FERMA (Federation of European Risk Management Associations)

4-3. Basel II was issued by the Basel Committee on Banking Supervision in 2004. It establishes risk and capital management rules designed to ensure that a bank holds capital reserves appropriate to the risk the bank exposes itself to through its lending and investment practices. Solvency II, developed by the European Commission in 2007, consists of regulatory requirements for insurance firms that operate in the European Union. It facilitated the development of a single market in insurance services in Europe while providing adequate consumer protection.

Direct Your Learning

ASSIGNMENT 6

Insurance as a Risk Management Technique

Educational Objectives

After learning the content of this assignment, you should be able to:

1. Explain how insurance reduces risk through pooling.
2. Explain how insurance benefits individuals, organizations, and society.
3. Explain why each of the six characteristics of an ideally insurable loss exposure is important to the insurance mechanism.
4. Explain how the six characteristics of an ideally insurable loss exposure apply to commercial loss exposures.
5. Explain how the six characteristics of an ideally insurable loss exposure apply to personal loss exposures.
6. Explain how state and federal governments are involved in the insurance market and the rationale for, and level of, their involvement.

Outline

- **How Insurance Reduces Risk**
  - A. Pooling
  - B. How Pooling Reduces Risk
  - C. How Insurance Uses Pooling
- **Benefits of Insurance**
  - A. Paying for Losses
  - B. Managing Cash Flow Uncertainty
  - C. Meeting Legal Requirements
  - D. Promoting Risk Control
  - E. Enabling Efficient Use of Resources
  - F. Providing Support for Insured's Credit
  - G. Providing Source of Investment Funds
  - H. Reducing Social Burdens
- **Characteristics of an Ideally Insurable Loss Exposure**
  - A. Pure Risk
  - B. Fortuitous
  - C. Definite and Measurable
    1. Definite
    2. Measurable
  - D. Large Number of Similar Exposure Units
    1. Cross-Sectional Risk Transfer
    2. Intertemporal Risk Transfer
  - E. Independent and Not Catastrophic
    1. Independent
    2. Not Catastrophic
  - F. Economically Feasible Premium
- **Insurability of Commercial Loss Exposures**
  - A. Property
    1. Fire
    2. Windstorm
    3. Flood
  - B. Liability
    1. Premises and Operations Liability
    2. Products Liability
  - C. Personnel
    1. Death
    2. Retirement
  - D. Net Income
    1. Net Income Loss Associated With Property Losses
    2. Net Income Loss Associated With Liability Losses
- **Insurability of Personal Loss Exposures**
  - A. Property
  - B. Liability
  - C. Net Income
  - D. Life, Health, and Retirement
    1. Life Loss Exposures
    2. Health Loss Exposures
    3. Retirement Loss Exposure
- **Government Insurance Programs**
  - A. Rationale for Government Involvement
    1. Fill Unmet Needs
    2. Compel Insurance Purchase
    3. Obtain Efficiency and Provide Convenience
    4. Achieve Collateral Social Purpose
  - B. Level of Government Involvement
    1. Exclusive Insurer
    2. Partner With Private Insurers
    3. Competitor to Private Insurers
  - C. Federal Compared With State Programs

s.m.a.r.t. tips

When you take the randomized full practice exams in the SMART Online Practice Exams product, you are seeing the same kinds of questions you will see when you take the actual exam. Take advantage of your time and learn the features of the software now.

For each assignment, you should define or describe each of the Key Words and Phrases and answer each of the Review and Application Questions.

Educational Objective 1

Explain how insurance reduces risk through pooling.

Review Questions

1-1. Describe the traits of an independent, or uncorrelated, loss exposure.

1-2. Describe the likelihood of extreme outcomes when using a pooling arrangement.

1-3. Describe the effect of pooling on the frequency of loss, severity of loss, and the probability distribution of losses.

Application Question

1-4. The Atwell Bus Corporation is a publicly held corporation providing school bus transportation to public and private schools in Midland County. Atwell owns 200 school buses, garaged in three different cities within the county. Its major competitors are two larger bus companies that operate in the same general area. School districts and private schools generally award contracts to the lowest bidder from among the bus companies, but they also consider overall performance and level of service in their evaluations.

a. Give one example of a correlated loss exposure faced by Atwell.

b. Give one example of an uncorrelated loss exposure faced by Atwell.

c. Suppose Atwell were to enter into a formal arrangement with the Green Bus Company, a similar company that operates in another state, to pool the losses suffered by both companies. How would this arrangement affect Atwell's risks with respect to each of the loss exposures you identified in a., above? Explain.

d. Suppose, instead, Atwell were to participate in a formal pool with fifteen other school bus companies. How, if at all, would this arrangement change your answer to b., above? Explain.

Educational Objective 2

Explain how insurance benefits individuals, organizations, and society.

Review Questions

2-1. List the ways insurance benefits individuals, organizations, and society.

2-2. Explain how an organization can achieve risk financing goals through the use of insurance.

2-3. List risk-sharing mechanisms an insurer may use to promote risk control.

Educational Objective 3

Explain why each of the six characteristics of an ideally insurable loss exposure is important to the insurance mechanism.

Key Word or Phrase

Fortuitous loss

Review Questions

3-1. Identify the six characteristics of an ideally insurable loss exposure.

3-2. Explain why insurance is designed to cover pure, not speculative, risk.

3-3. Identify the factors an insurer must be able to determine for a loss exposure to be definite in time, cause, and location.

▶▶

3-4. Describe the types of losses an insurer might consider uninsurable because the premium charged would not be economically feasible.

Educational Objective 4

Explain how the six characteristics of an ideally insurable loss exposure apply to commercial loss exposures.

Review Questions

4-1. Explain whether the building that houses an organization's main operations would meet the six ideally insurable characteristics for the following causes of loss:

a. Fire

b. Windstorm

c. Flood

4-2. Describe two common sources of liability risk faced by many commercial organizations.

4-3. Compare the insurability of personnel losses caused by an employee's death and those caused by an employee's retirement.

Application Question

4-4. Shore Point Mall is a mall of sixty retail stores located along the Outer Banks of North Carolina's shoreline. Outer Banks Insurance Company, a small local property insurer that insures more than 40 percent of properties in the Outer Banks area, is considering selling a commercial property policy to Shore Point Mall that includes coverage for windstorm damage. Determine whether Shore Point Mall exhibits all six characteristics of an ideally insurable loss exposure for windstorm damage.

Educational Objective 5

Explain how the six characteristics of an ideally insurable loss exposure apply to personal loss exposures.

Review Questions

5-1. Identify common sources of liability risk faced by individuals.

5-2. For purposes of life insurance, identify individual circumstances that may prevent insurers from offering an economically feasible premium.

5-3. Explain why retirement does not usually exhibit the fortuitous characteristics of ideally insurable loss exposures.

Educational Objective 6

Explain how state and federal governments are involved in the insurance market and the rationale for, and level of, their involvement.

Review Questions

6-1. Identify reasons for government involvement in insurance.

6-2. Explain how the government provides incentives for the purchase of insurance.

6-3. Identify three levels of governmental participation in governmental insurance programs.

6-4. Explain how state or federal governmental involvement in insurance programs is determined.

Application Question

6-5. The Pennsylvania state insurance commissioner is concerned that the state's workers compensation insurance market is not competitive. Only a few insurers are selling workers compensation in Pennsylvania, and rates are high relative to many other comparable states. Describe some of the considerations the insurance commissioner should take into account before recommending that the state become involved in providing workers compensation insurance to employers in Pennsylvania.

Answers to Assignment 6 Questions

NOTE: These answers are provided to give students a basic understanding of acceptable types of responses. They often are not the only valid answers and are not intended to provide an exhaustive response to the questions.

Educational Objective 1

1-1. A loss exposure is considered independent (uncorrelated with any others) when a loss at one loss exposure has no effect on the probability of a loss at another loss exposure.

1-2. As the number of participants in the pool grows, extreme outcomes become less likely at the pool level.

1-3. Pooling does not change the frequency or severity of an individual loss exposure, but it does change the probability distribution of the loss because the sources of the loss exposures and the resources to pay for losses have been combined. The result is that the uncertainty around the expected value has decreased.

1-4.

a. An example of a correlated loss exposure is a bus breakdown caused by a defective design in Atwell's buses.

b. An example of an uncorrelated loss exposure is a serious bus accident resulting in multiple deaths.

c. The arrangement with Green would have the following effects on Atwell's loss exposures:

   i. The correlated loss exposure—Assuming both Atwell's and Green's fleets included buses with the same defect (perfectly positively correlated loss), the risks would be unchanged. If losses are not perfectly positively correlated, some risk could be reduced through pooling, although the magnitude is less than with uncorrelated losses.

   ii. The uncorrelated loss exposure—Although the number of serious accidents for which Atwell would be required to share resources with Green would increase, Atwell's share of the losses would become more predictable, reducing Atwell's risks.

d. A pool with fifteen other school bus companies would further reduce Atwell's risks involving uncorrelated loss exposures.

Educational Objective 2

2-1. Insurance benefits individuals, organizations, and society in the following ways:

- Indemnifies individuals and organizations for covered losses
- Enables individuals and organizations to manage cash flow uncertainty
- Enables individuals and organizations to meet legal requirements
- Promotes risk control
- Frees up insured's financial resources for other expenditures or investments
- Supports insured's credit
- Provides source of investment funds for insurers and insureds
- Helps reduces social burden

2-2. Insurance helps an organization achieve risk financing goals in the following ways:

- Indemnifies for covered losses—Insurance indemnifies the insured, subject to applicable deductibles and policy limits, for losses to covered loss exposures resulting from covered causes of loss.
- Manages cash flow uncertainty—Insurance helps reduce the financial effect on the insured's cash flow to any deductible payments and any loss amounts that exceed the policy limits.
- Meets legal requirements—Insurance is often used or required to satisfy statutory requirements and contractual requirements that arise from business relationships.

2-3. The following risk-sharing mechanisms promote risk control:

- Deductibles
- Premium credit incentives
- Contractual requirements

Educational Objective 3

3-1. The six characteristics of an ideally insurable loss exposure are as follows:

- Pure risk
- Fortuitous losses
- Definite and measurable
- Large number of similar exposure units
- Independent and not catastrophic
- Affordable

3-2. Insurance is designed to cover pure, not speculative, risk because the purpose of insurance is to indemnify the insured for a loss, not to enable the insured to profit from the loss. If the loss exposure has a possibility of gain, the insurance premium the insurer would have to charge would offset the potential gain.

3-3. An insurer must be able to determine the following to consider a loss exposure definite in time, cause, and location:

- The event that led up to the loss
- When that event or series of events occurred
- Where that event occurred

3-4. Losses an insurer might consider uninsurable because the premium charged would not be economically feasible are those involving only low-severity losses and those involving a high frequency of loss.

Educational Objective 4

4-1. The building that houses an organization's main operations meets the six ideally insurable characteristics for these causes of loss in the following ways:

a. For most property loss exposures, the main underwriting criteria focus on the threat of loss by fire. Commercial property loss exposures associated with fire generally meet all six characteristics. An exception would be arson-for-profit.

b. Windstorm damage to commercial property loss exposures is generally a pure risk subject to fortuitous losses that are definite and measurable. However, it may not meet the last three ideally insurable characteristics: large number of similar exposure units (depends on property location, property type, and use), independent and not catastrophic, premiums economically feasible.

c. Flood generally involves pure risk and losses that are fortuitous, definite, and measurable. The main issue is that the flood cause of loss is geographically concentrated, so loss exposures tend not to be independent, and losses could be catastrophic from the insurer's perspective. As a result, flood loss premiums are high and flood can be economically unfeasible to insure for some organizations.

4-2. Among sources of liability risk faced by many commercial organizations are the following two:

- Premises and operations liability—liability because of bodily injury or property damage caused by an accident on owned or rented premises or away from the premises if it arises out of the organization's ongoing operations
- Products liability—liability because of bodily injury or property damage resulting from defective or inherently dangerous products

4-3. Personnel losses caused by an employee's death generally exhibit the six characteristics of an ideally insurable loss exposure. Such a loss exposure involves pure risk that is fortuitous, independent, and not catastrophic, and that is usually economically feasible to insure.

Personnel losses caused by an employee's retirement do not meet the six characteristics of an ideally insurable loss exposure because retirement is usually planned (not a fortuitous loss) and because the loss may not be economically feasible to insure.

▶▶

4-4. Shore Point Mall does meet the first three characteristics for windstorm damage. Windstorm is a pure risk, fortuitous, and definite and measurable. Because the mall is a retail mall, it probably does meet the fourth characteristic of being a large number of similar exposure units. However, from Outer Banks Insurance Company's perspective, the windstorm cause of loss is probably not independent and not catastrophic. Outer Banks Insurance has insured a large percentage of the local market, and a major hurricane would affect a large percentage of its insureds. This may make it difficult for Outer Banks Insurance to charge a feasible premium and still maintain its claim-paying ability.

Educational Objective 5

5-1. Individuals face the following common sources of liability risk:

- Real property ownership (premises) liability loss exposures
- Automobile liability loss exposures

5-2. Individual circumstances, such as health conditions or hazardous occupations, may prevent insurers from offering an economically feasible premium.

5-3. Retirement does not usually exhibit the fortuitous characteristics of ideally insurable loss exposures because the individual has control over savings and choice of retirement dates.

Educational Objective 6

6-1. Government involvement in insurance occurs for the following reasons:

- To fulfill insurance needs unmet by private insurers
- To compel people to buy a particular type of insurance
- To obtain greater efficiency and/or provide convenience to insurance buyers
- To achieve collateral social purposes

6-2. The government provides incentives for the purchase of insurance through a combination of regulation and provision of insurance at a reasonable price.

6-3. Governmental participation in governmental insurance programs includes the following three levels:

- Exclusive insurer
- Partner with private insurers
- Competitor to private insurers

6-4. One consideration relating to whether state or federal government should be involved in insurance programs may be that if the rationale for government involvement extends beyond state boundaries or would affect interstate commerce, the federal government should be running the insurance program.

6-5. The Pennsylvania insurance commissioner should consider why the state needs to be involved in the workers compensation insurance market. It appears that the rationale is to fill insurance needs unmet by private insurers (provide insurance at an affordable rate) or to obtain greater efficiency in the market (increase competition)—the two major reasons the state should be involved. Another possible rationale is to facilitate compulsory purchase of workers compensation insurance by making it available at a reasonable cost. The commissioner needs to determine how the state would be involved—as the exclusive insurer, as a partner with private insurers, or as a competitor to private insurers.

Direct Your Learning

ASSIGNMENT 7

Insurance Policy Analysis

Educational Objectives

After learning the content of this assignment, you should be able to:

1. Describe the following characteristics of insurance policies, including common exceptions to these characteristics:
   - Indemnity
   - Utmost good faith
   - Fortuitous losses
   - Contract of adhesion
   - Exchange of unequal amounts
   - Conditional
   - Nontransferable
2. Describe these approaches to insurance policy structure and how they can affect policy analysis:
   - Self-contained and modular policies
   - Preprinted and manuscript policies
   - Standard and nonstandard forms
   - Endorsements and other related documents
3. Describe the purpose(s) and characteristics of each of these types of policy provisions in a property-casualty insurance policy:
   - Declarations
   - Definitions
   - Insuring agreements
   - Exclusions
   - Conditions

7 ASSIGNMENT

Educational Objectives, continued

- Miscellaneous provisions

4. Describe the primary methods of insurance policy analysis.

Outline

- **Distinguishing Characteristics of Insurance Policies**
  - A. Indemnity
    - 1. Insurance Should Not Overindemnify
    - 2. Insureds Should Not Be Indemnified More Than Once per Loss
  - B. Utmost Good Faith
  - C. Fortuitous Losses
  - D. Contract of Adhesion
  - E. Exchange of Unequal Amounts
  - F. Conditional
  - G. Nontransferable
- **Structure of Insurance Policies**
  - A. Self-Contained and Modular Policies
  - B. Preprinted and Manuscript Forms
  - C. Standard and Nonstandard Forms
  - D. Endorsements and Other Related Documents
- **Policy Provisions**
  - A. Declarations
  - B. Definitions
  - C. Insuring Agreements
  - D. Exclusions
    - 1. Eliminate Coverage for Uninsurable Loss Exposures
    - 2. Assist in Managing Moral and Morale Hazards
    - 3. Reduce Likelihood of Coverage Duplications
    - 4. Eliminate Coverages Not Needed by the Typical Insured
    - 5. Eliminate Coverages Requiring Special Treatment
    - 6. Assist in Keeping Premiums Reasonable
  - E. Conditions
  - F. Miscellaneous Provisions
- **Policy Analysis**
  - A. Pre-Loss Policy Analysis
  - B. Post-Loss Policy Analysis

study tips

Set aside a specific, realistic amount of time to study every day.

For each assignment, you should define or describe each of the Key Words and Phrases and answer each of the Review and Application Questions.

Educational Objective 1

Describe the following characteristics of insurance policies, including common exceptions to these characteristics:

- **Indemnity**
- **Utmost good faith**
- **Fortuitous losses**
- **Contract of adhesion**
- **Exchange of unequal amounts**
- **Conditional**
- **Nontransferable**

Key Words and Phrases

Principle of indemnity

Contract of indemnity

Collateral source rule

Contract of adhesion

Reasonable expectations doctrine

Consideration

Conditional contract

Review Questions

1-1. List the distinguishing characteristics of an insurance policy.

1-2. Identify reasons that an insurance policy might not fully indemnify an insured after a covered loss.

1-3. Explain the distinction between a contract of indemnity and a valued policy.

1-4. Identify two policy characteristics that help an insurer reduce or avoid moral hazards associated with indemnification.

1-5. Identify two reasons an insurance policy might be vulnerable to misrepresentation or opportunism and how the concept of utmost good faith helps prevent occurrences of such abuses.

1-6. Explain why insurance is not intended for losses that are not fortuitous.

1-7. Identify factors courts consider when determining whether to classify an insured as a sophisticated insured.

1-8. Explain how an insurer makes certain that the tangible consideration offered by the insured in an insurance contract is equitable.

▶▶

1-9. Explain why insurance policies are conditional contracts.

Application Questions

1-10. Tony was bragging to his new neighbors about how little he paid for his auto insurance for his sixteen-year-old son, who has been ticketed for speeding three times in the last two months. When one neighbor asked how he was able to buy insurance for such a low premium, Tony replied that he told the insurer that his son is twenty-five years old and has a perfect driving record. The neighbor asked Tony if he thought that what he was doing was wrong. Tony responded, "No, I've been paying premiums for twenty years without a claim. I'm just getting a discount they owe me anyway." Which of the distinguishing characteristics of insurance policies is Tony's policy missing?

1-11. Millwright Art Museum (MAM) paid $5 million at a June auction for the only known painting by Cassandra Cole, a famous nineteenth century sculptor. MAM insured the painting under a valued policy for $5.1 million with Art Insurance Company, which renewed the policy the following June. On August 1, more than fifty paintings by Cole were discovered in a storage area at a European museum. That September, a fire destroyed the wing of the MAM where the Cole painting was on display. The market value of the original Cole painting at the time of the loss was only $1 million. Should Art Insurance pay the full $5.1 million valued policy? Would that payment violate the principle of indemnity?

Educational Objective 2

Describe these approaches to insurance policy structure and how they can affect policy analysis:

- **Self-contained and modular policies**
- **Preprinted and manuscript policies**
- **Standard and nonstandard forms**
- **Endorsements and other related documents**

Key Words and Phrases

Self-contained policy

Monoline policy

Package policy

Modular policy

Manuscript form

Review Questions

2-1. Identify the advantages of modular policies, relative to self-contained policies.

2-2. Explain why insurance and risk management professionals might find policy analysis more difficult with multiple self-contained policies than with a single modular policy.

2-3. Differentiate between preprinted and manuscript forms.

2-4. Identify the types of related documents that might become part of and alter an insurance policy by being attached to or referenced within the policy.

2-5. List two general policy interpretation rules that are applied when an endorsement conflicts with the policy to which it is attached.

Application Question

2-6. Eileen, the owner of a high-rise office complex in New York City, has been negotiating with a consortium of insurers to design a property insurance program to provide enough coverage for her multi-billion-dollar property. Eileen was not satisfied with the wording of the flood exclusion on the standard form the insurers wanted to use, so she negotiated the wording of the exclusion with the insurers. While the policy was in force, Eileen's property was damaged when a water tower on the roof of the building ruptured and poured millions of gallons of water through the building. Eileen's insurer denied the claim based on the wording of the flood exclusion. Eileen's broker told her not to worry because in court cases involving the standard flood exclusion, the courts have "always found for the insured" in similar situations. Is Eileen's broker correct in telling Eileen not to worry? Will the courts side with her? Why or why not?

Educational Objective 3

Describe the purpose(s) and characteristics of each of these types of policy provisions in a property-casualty insurance policy:

- **Declarations**
- **Definitions**
- **Insuring agreements**
- **Exclusions**
- **Conditions**
- **Miscellaneous provisions**

Key Words and Phrases

Declarations page (declarations, or dec.)

Insuring agreement

Exclusion

Policy condition

Review Questions

3-1. Describe the six common policy provisions contained in an insurance policy.

3-2. Explain the distinction between coverage provided by named perils and that provided by special-form commercial property insurance.

3-3. Identify loss exposures typically excluded from a policy because they are considered uninsurable.

Educational Objective 4

Describe the primary methods of insurance policy analysis.

Review Questions

4-1. Describe the sources of information insureds may use to generate scenarios for pre-loss policy analysis.

4-2. Describe a limitation of scenario analysis.

4-3. Describe the primary method of post-loss policy analysis.

Application Question

4-4. A family's home is destroyed by a fire. Explain how a claims adjuster for the home's insurer could determine whether the loss was covered by the family's homeowners policy.

Answers to Assignment 7 Questions

NOTE: These answers are provided to give students a basic understanding of acceptable types of responses. They often are not the only valid answers and are not intended to provide an exhaustive response to the questions.

Educational Objective 1

1-1. The following are the seven distinguishing characteristics of an insurance policy:

- Indemnity
- Utmost good faith
- Fortuitous losses
- Contract of adhesion
- Exchange of unequal amounts
- Conditional
- Nontransferable

1-2. An insurance policy might not fully indemnify an insured after a covered loss because most insurance policies contain a dollar limit, a deductible, or other provisions or limitations on the amount to be paid.

1-3. A contract of indemnity compensates the insured only for the value of the loss. In a valued insurance policy, the insurer agrees to pay a preestablished dollar amount in the event of an insured total loss, which may overindemnify or underindemnify the insured.

1-4. In order to reduce or avoid moral hazards associated with indemnification, an insurance policy should not do the following:

- Overindemnify the insured
- Indemnify insureds more than once per loss

1-5. An insurance policy may be vulnerable to misrepresentation or opportunism for two reasons.

These situations could affect underwriting decisions and lead to adverse selection. The concept of utmost good faith obligates all parties to act with complete honesty and to disclose all relevant facts and therefore helps prevent these situations.

- One party to a contract has information the other party does not (information asymmetry).
- The costly verification of information may lead an insurer to fail to verify information provided by the insured.

1-6. Insurance is not intended for losses that are not fortuitous because if an insured knows of a loss in advance and the insurer does not, the insured has an information advantage over the insurer. This situation promotes adverse selection, thereby increasing the losses in the pool the insurer insures.

1-7. The factors a court may consider to determine whether an insured is a sophisticated insured include the following:

- Size of the insured organization
- Size of the organization's risk management department
- Use of an insurance broker or legal counsel with expertise in insurance policies
- Relative bargaining power of the insured in relation to the insurer

1-8. An insurer makes sure that the tangible consideration exchanged by the insured for an insurance contract is equitable by charging a premium that is directly proportional to the insured's expected losses on an actuarially sound basis.

1-9. Insurance policies are conditional contracts because the insurer is obligated to pay for losses incurred by the insured only if the insured has fulfilled all of the policy conditions.

1-10. Tony's policy fails to exhibit utmost good faith. Utmost good faith requires that a person applying for insurance make a full and fair disclosure of the risk presented by the loss exposures to be insured.

1-11. Valued policies can violate the principle of indemnity by underinsuring or overinsuring a particular loss exposure. In this case, Art Insurance would still pay the full $5.1 million because the policy was in force at the time of the loss and the painting was destroyed in the fire. The payment would violate the principle of indemnity.

Educational Objective 2

2-1. The advantages of using modular policies, relative to self-contained policies, include the following:

- Carefully designed and coordinated provisions in the various forms minimize the possibility of gaps and overlaps.
- Consistent terminology, definitions, and policy language make coverage interpretation easier for the insured.
- Fewer forms are required to meet a wide range of needs.
- Underwriting is simplified because much of the basic information that must be analyzed applies to all lines of insurance.
- Adverse selection problems can be reduced.
- Insurers often give a package discount when several coverages are included in the same policy.

2-2. Insurance and risk management professionals might find policy analysis more difficult with multiple self-contained policies than with a single modular policy for these reasons:

- Multiple self-contained policies often use inconsistent terminology and have gaps and overlaps in coverage.
- Modular policies offer a better framework for policy analysis.

2-3. Most insurance policies are assembled from one or more preprinted forms, which are designed to be used by many insureds. The forms themselves are not altered or customized for each insured. Manuscript forms are unique forms developed through negotiation between the insurer and insured. Preprinted standard forms are the easiest forms to evaluate during policy analysis because they are widely used and more consistently interpreted by the courts and because insurance professionals generally have more experience working with these forms. Manuscript forms are the most difficult forms to interpret because they often contain unique wording and can vary widely in their interpretation.

2-4. These documents may become part of an insurance policy by being attached to or referenced within the policy:

- Endorsements—Endorsements are added to modify a basic policy form. Policies in several lines of business have "standard" endorsements that are included in most of the policies written in that line.
- Completed application—In some jurisdictions, statutes require that any written application be made part of the policy for certain lines of insurance.
- Insurer's bylaws—With certain types of policies, such as those with mutual or reciprocal insurers, the insurer's bylaws regarding rights and duties are specified in the policy.
- Insurer's rating manual—Some policies incorporate the insurer's rating manual by referring to it in the policy language.
- Other documents—Some frequently incorporated documents include premium notes, inspection reports, and specification sheets or operating manuals relating to safety equipment or procedures.

2-5. The following two policy interpretation rules apply when an endorsement contradicts the policy to which it is attached:

a. An endorsement takes precedence over any conflicting terms in the policy.

b. A handwritten endorsement supersedes a computer-printed or typewritten one.

2-6. Eileen should be worried. Her broker's comment that "courts always side with the insured" applies to the standard flood exclusion, which is an example of a contract of adhesion. However, Eileen negotiated the wording of the flood exclusion, which makes this policy a manuscript policy. Manuscript policies, because the insured participated in determining the wording of the policy, are not generally considered contracts of adhesion. Therefore, the court's interpretation of the standard flood exclusion may not be relevant to Eileen's case. The courts may or may not side with Eileen in answering the question of coverage in this manuscript policy.

Educational Objective 3

3-1. The following six policy provisions are commonly contained in an insurance policy:

a. Declarations—contain information regarding who or what is covered, and where and when coverage applies.

b. Definitions—define terms used throughout the entire policy or form.

▶▶

c. Insuring agreements—state for each line of insurance offered in the policy that the insurer will, under certain circumstances, make a payment or provide a service.

d. Exclusions—state what the insurer does not intend to cover, thereby limiting coverage and clarifying the coverages granted by the insurer.

e. Conditions—qualify an otherwise enforceable promise of the insurer. Examples are the insured's obligation to pay premiums, report losses promptly, provide appropriate documentation for losses, cooperate with the insurer in any legal proceedings, and refrain from jeopardizing an insurer's rights to recover from responsible third parties.

f. Miscellaneous provisions—deal with the relationship between the insured and the insurer or help to establish working procedures for implementing the policy.

3-2. Coverage provided by named perils and special-form commercial property insurance differs as follows:

- A named perils policy restricts coverage to the perils (causes of loss) identified in the policy.
- A special-form policy provides protection against perils that the form does not specifically exclude.

3-3. The following loss exposures are typically excluded from a policy because they are considered uninsurable:

- War
- Criminal acts committed by the insured
- Normal wear and tear

Educational Objective 4

4-1. For insureds, the primary source of information for generating scenarios for pre-loss policy analysis is their past loss experience. If the insured has not experienced a loss that triggered insurance coverage, friends, neighbors, co-workers, and family members can provide information about their experiences with losses and the claim process. The insurance producer and customer service representative are also good sources of information.

4-2. One of the limitations of scenario analysis is that, because the number of possible loss scenarios is theoretically infinite, it is impossible to account for every possibility.

4-3. The primary method of post-loss policy analysis is the DICE (an acronym representing the policy provision categories: declarations, insuring agreements, conditions, and exclusions) method, which is a systematic review of all the categories of property-casualty policy provisions.

4-4. The claims adjuster would follow the steps specified in the DICE decision tree to determine whether the family's homeowners policy covered the loss.

First, he or she would check the declarations to see whether anything there would preclude coverage. If not, he or she would go to the next step.

Second, he or she would see whether anything in the insuring agreement would preclude coverage. If not, he or she would go to the next step.

Third, he or she would check the conditions to see whether anything precluded coverage and, if not, go to the next step.

Fourth, he or she would check the exclusions and all other policy provisions not already analyzed, including the endorsements and miscellaneous provisions, to make sure that nothing would preclude coverage. If not, he or she would determine the amount payable under the policy.

Direct Your Learning

ASSIGNMENT 8

Common Policy Concepts

Educational Objectives

After learning the content of this assignment, you should be able to:

1. Given a case, evaluate one or more entities' insurable interests.
2. Explain why insurance to value is important to property insurers, how insurers encourage insurance to value, and what insureds can do to address the problems associated with maintaining insurance to value.
3. Explain how property is valued under each of the following valuation methods in property insurance policies:
   - Actual cash value
   - Replacement cost
   - Agreed value
   - Functional valuation
4. Explain how the amount payable for a claim covered under a liability insurance policy is determined.
5. Explain how deductibles in property insurance benefit the insured.
6. Explain why deductibles are not commonly used in some liability policies but are commonly used in other liability policies, and how a self-insured retention differs from a deductible.
7. Describe the multiple sources of recovery that may be available to an insurance policyholder for a covered loss.

Outline

- **Insurable Interest**
  - A. When and Why Insurable Interest Is Required
  - B. Legal Bases for Insurable Interest
    1. Ownership Interest in Property
    2. Contractual Obligations
    3. Exposure to Legal Liability
    4. Factual Expectancy
    5. Representation of Another Party
  - C. Multiple Parties With Insurable Interests
    1. Joint Tenancy
    2. Tenancy by the Entirety
    3. Tenancy in Common
    4. Tenancy in Partnership
- **Insurance to Value**
  - A. Why Insurers Seek Insurance to Value
  - B. How Insurers Encourage Insurance to Value
  - C. Addressing Insurance-to-Value Problems
- **Property Valuation Methods**
  - A. Actual Cash Value
    1. Replacement Cost Minus Depreciation
    2. Market Value
    3. Broad Evidence Rule
  - B. Replacement Cost
  - C. Other Valuation Methods
    1. Agreed Value Method
    2. Functional Valuation Method
- **Valuation of Liability Claims**
  - A. Compensable Amount of the Claim
    1. Settlement of the Claim
    2. Extent of Damages
  - B. Policy Limits
- **Reasons for Property Insurance Deductibles**
  - A. Encourage Risk Control
  - B. Reduce Insurer's Costs
- **Liability Deductibles and Self-Insured Retentions**
  - A. Reasons for Limited Use
  - B. Self-Insured Retentions
- **Other Sources of Recovery**
  - A. Noninsurance Agreements
  - B. Negligent Third Parties
  - C. Other Insurance in the Same Policy
  - D. Other Insurance in a Similar Policy
  - E. Other Insurance in Dissimilar Policies

Plan to register with The Institutes well in advance of your exam. For complete information regarding exam dates and fees, please visit our Web page, www.TheInstitutes.org/forms, where you can access and print exam registration information.

For each assignment, you should define or describe each of the Key Words and Phrases and answer each of the Review and Application Questions.

Educational Objective 1

Given a case, evaluate one or more entities' insurable interests.

Key Words and Phrases

Insurable interest

Factual expectancy

Agent

Trustee

Bailee

Bailor

Application Questions

1-1. Danford Hospital has hired Surewell Construction Management as an agent to solicit bids from construction firms for building a parking garage on the hospital's premises and to handle all communications with the construction firm selected. Surewell has awarded the bid for construction to Zelles Construction Company. Danford has signed a construction loan contract and ultimate mortgage commitment with Etchley Financial. Zelles has begun construction of the garage. The new parking garage is being constructed in the location of the former employee parking lot. During the construction, employees of Danford Hospital must park in an overflow parking lot one block from the hospital.

For each of the following, indicate whether that entity has an insurable interest in the parking garage by answering "yes" or "no" and, if answering "yes," describe the basis for that interest.

a. Danford Hospital

b. Surewell Construction Management

c. Zelles Construction

▶▶

d. Etchley Financial

e. Danford Hospital employees

1-2. Charles and Ramona are husband and wife. They have tenancy by entirety in their home at 9000 Swales Road, valued at $350,000. Before they were married, Ramona took tenancy in common in an apartment building valued at $2 million at 2011 Tyler Street with her three sisters, Deb, Rachel, and Donelle. The four women owned equal shares of the building. Ramona died in an accident.

For each of the following, indicate who has an insurable interest after Ramona's death and what the value of those interests is.

a. Home at 9000 Swales Road

b. Apartment building at 2011 Tyler Street

Educational Objective 2

Explain why insurance to value is important to property insurers, how insurers encourage insurance to value, and what insureds can do to address the problems associated with maintaining insurance to value.

Key Words and Phrases

Insurance to value

Loss frequency

Loss severity

Insurance-to-value provision

Coinsurance clause

Agreed value optional coverage

Inflation guard protection

Peak season endorsement

▶▶

Review Questions

2-1. In what two ways does an insurer benefit when property is insured to value?

2-2. How do coinsurance clauses encourage commercial property insureds to insure their property to value?

2-3. What are two reasons why insureds have difficulty maintaining property insurance limits that meet or exceed coinsurance requirements or the insurance-to-value requirement?

Educational Objective 3

Explain how property is valued under each of the following valuation methods in property insurance policies:

- **Actual cash value**
- **Replacement cost**
- **Agreed value**
- **Functional valuation**

Key Words and Phrases

Actual cash value (ACV)

Replacement cost

Market value

Broad evidence rule

Agreed value method

Functional valuation method

Review Questions

3-1. Describe three common methods of determining ACV for property.

3-2. Describe the types of property for which market valuation may be useful.

3-3. Explain why the value of land must be eliminated when determining values for buildings or structures on that land.

3-4. Identify the factors considered when determining a building's ACV under the broad evidence rule.

3-5. Explain how insurers reduce the potential moral hazard related to offering coverage on a replacement cost basis.

3-6. Explain why the functional valuation method might be used for some types of property.

3-7. Describe the types of personal property for which the functional valuation method is commonly used.

Educational Objective 4

Explain how the amount payable for a claim covered under a liability insurance policy is determined.

Key Word or Phrase

Damages

Review Questions

4-1. Explain how the compensable amount of the claim is determined under a liability insurance policy.

4-2. Describe the factors that determine the extent of damages related to each of the following types of claim.

a. Property damage claim

b. Bodily injury claim

4-3. Explain how the maximum amount payable for a covered claim is determined in a liability policy that contains multiple policy limits.

Application Questions

4-4. An insured with a CGL policy incurs a covered claim for $500,000 in damages. The policy has a $1 million each occurrence limit. Prior claims paid during the same policy period reduced the applicable aggregate limit to $100,000. Explain how the insurer's payment is affected by these facts.

4-5. An insured has a directors and officers liability policy with a $1 million policy limit. The insured is held liable for a $975,000 judgment and defense costs totaling $150,000. Determine the insurer's payment based on the following scenarios:

a. The defense costs and supplementary payment reduce the policy limits.

b. The liability policy covers defense costs in addition to the policy limits.

Educational Objective 5

Explain how deductibles in property insurance benefit the insured.

Key Word or Phrase

Dollar trading

Review Questions

5-1. Explain how the size of a deductible can affect the insured's risk control incentive to prevent or reduce losses.

5-2. Explain how deductibles affect premiums for insurers and insureds.

5-3. Explain how medium-sized deductibles affect premium credits.

Educational Objective 6

Explain why deductibles are not commonly used in some liability policies but are commonly used in other liability policies, and how a self-insured retention differs from a deductible.

Key Word or Phrase

Self-insured retention (SIR)

Review Questions

6-1. Describe the effectiveness of deductibles in liability insurance policies.

6-2. Compare deductibles and self-insured retentions.

Educational Objective 7

Describe the multiple sources of recovery that may be available to an insurance policyholder for a covered loss.

Review Questions

7-1. List the five other sources of recovery that liability insurance policy provisions address.

7-2. Explain how subrogation addresses negligent third parties and the rights to recovery.

7-3. Explain how duplicate coverage may arise in a package policy.

▶▶

Answers to Assignment 8 Questions

NOTE: These answers are provided to give students a basic understanding of acceptable types of responses. They often are not the only valid answers and are not intended to provide an exhaustive response to the questions.

Educational Objective 1

1-1.

a. Yes. Danford has an ownership interest in the parking garage.

b. Yes. Surewell has an agent interest in the parking garage as a representative of Danford.

c. Yes. Zelles has a contractual obligation to Danford and Surewell that creates an interest in the parking garage.

d. Yes. Etchley has a contractual obligation with Danford that creates an interest (as secured creditor) in the parking garage.

e. No.

1-2.

a. Charles would have insurable interest in the full $350,000 value of the home.

b. Deb, Rachel, and Donelle would each have an insurable interest in one-fourth of the apartment building's value, or $500,000 each. Ramona's $500,000 share would pass to her heirs.

Educational Objective 2

2-1. When property is insured to value, the insurer benefits because (1) the premium is adequate to cover potential losses and (2) it simplifies the underwriting process by reducing the need to determine exact values during underwriting.

2-2. Coinsurance clauses encourage commercial property insureds to insure their property to value by making the insured responsible for retaining part of any loss if the property is underinsured below some specified percentage of the property's insurable value.

2-3. Two reasons that insureds have difficulty maintaining appropriate property limits include these (only two required):

- The amount of insurance necessary to meet coinsurance requirements is based on the insured property's value at the time of the loss, but the policy limit is selected when the policy is purchased.
- When selecting insurance limits, an insurance buyer typically estimates property values based on an informed guess.
- The insurable value at the time of the loss often cannot be precisely measured until the property is actually rebuilt or replaced.
- Values change over time.

Educational Objective 3

3-1. The following are three common methods of determining ACV for property:

- Replacement cost minus depreciation.
- Market value. Many courts have ruled that ACV means market value, the price at which a particular piece of property could be sold on the open market by an unrelated buyer and seller.
- The broad evidence rule. Actual cash value is determined based on court decisions that require all relevant factors to be considered.

3-2. Market valuation may be useful when property of like kind and quality is unavailable for purchase, such as with antiques, works of art, and other collectibles. These types of property may be irreplaceable, making replacement cost calculations impossible. Market valuation can also be the most accurate way to determine the value of some older or historic buildings built with obsolete construction methods and materials.

3-3. Because most insurance policies cover buildings and structures but not land, the land's value must be eliminated in establishing insurable values of property.

3-4. When the broad evidence rule is used to determine a building's ACV, the following factors are considered:

- Obsolescence
- Building's present use and profitability
- Alternate building uses
- Present neighborhood characteristics
- Long-term community plans for the area where the building is located, including urban renewal prospects and new roadway plans
- Inflationary or deflationary trends

3-5. To reduce the moral hazard, most replacement cost policies pay out only after the insured has actually replaced the damaged or destroyed property or, in some cases, only if the loss is a relatively low value. In many policies with replacement cost provisions, the insured has the option of settling the claim based on ACV and then has 180 days to refile the claim on the replacement cost basis. This gives the insured the opportunity to obtain funds from the insurer at the time of loss, use those funds to help pay for the rebuilding, and then collect the full replacement cost value on completion.

3-6. The functional valuation method is sometimes used when replacing buildings or personal property with property of like kind and quality is not practical and when the ACV method does not match insurance needs.

3-7. The functional valuation method is commonly used with electronics and computers, because new computers may be more functional but less expensive than the models that have to be replaced.

Educational Objective 4

4-1. The compensable amount of the claim is determined by negotiations between the liability insurer and the claimant if the claim can be settled out of court. If a settlement cannot be reached by the parties involved, the liability claim will go to trial, and the extent of the insured's liability to the claimant is then based on legal principles.

4-2.

a. The owner may recover the reasonable cost to repair the property or replace the property if it cannot be economically repaired. When the property must be replaced, the owner is entitled to the property's reasonable market value before damage or destruction and may also recover damages to compensate for the loss of use of the property.

b. A broader range of factors applies, including the following:

- Reasonable and necessary medical expenses
- Type of bodily injury
- Lost wages and loss of earning capacity
- Other out-of-pocket expenses, such as household assistance
- Current and future pain and suffering resulting from the bodily injury
- Extent and permanency of disability and impairment
- Disfigurement resulting from bodily injury
- Preexisting conditions that could have contributed to the bodily injury

4-3. When a liability policy contains multiple limits, the maximum amount payable for a covered claim depends on a complete analysis of the interactions among the various limits.

4-4. Because prior claims paid during the same policy period reduced the applicable aggregate limit to $100,000, the insurer's payment will not exceed $100,000.

4-5.

a. If an insured with a $1 million policy limit were held liable for a $975,000 judgment and defense costs totaling $150,000, the insurer would pay only $850,000 of the judgment after having paid the defense costs.

b. If the insured had a liability policy that covered defense costs in addition to the limits, the insurer would pay both the $150,000 in defense costs and the $975,000 judgment in full.

Educational Objective 5

5-1. A deductible should be large enough to have a noticeable financial effect on the insured. Deductibles that are too small do not offer enough financial incentive, and deductibles that are too large defeat the purpose of transferring the loss exposure to the insurer.

5-2. Deductibles reduce the premiums insurers must charge and ultimately benefit the insured in the following ways:

- Reduce insurers' overall loss costs and loss adjustment expenses
- Provide insureds with risk control incentives
- Reduce the morale and moral hazard incentive

5-3. Premium credits tend to encourage the use of medium-sized deductibles that eliminate dollar trading for small losses but that provide a reliable source of recovery for large losses.

Educational Objective 6

6-1. Deductibles in liability policies are not as effective as they are in property insurance policies. Liability insurers want to control liability claims from the outset; therefore, they want to be involved in even small liability claims that may be less than the deductible amount. In addition, for most liability policies, deductibles would not noticeably reduce premiums because relatively few liability claims involve small amounts that an insurer would be able to avoid with a deductible. Finally, the insurer generally has to pay the third-party claimant the full settlement amount and then try to collect the deductible from the insured, who may be unwilling or unable to make the payment.

6-2. The differences between a deductible and a self-insured retention (SIR) are as follows:

- With a liability insurance deductible, the insurer defends on a first-dollar basis, pays all covered losses, and then bills the insured for the amount of losses up to the deductible.
- With an SIR, the insurer pays only losses that exceed the SIR amount. The insurer does not defend claims below the SIR amount. Consequently, the organization is responsible for adjusting and paying its own losses up to the SIR amount.

Educational Objective 7

7-1. The five other sources of recovery that liability insurance policy provisions address can include these:

- Noninsurance agreements
- Negligent third parties
- Other insurance in the same policy
- Other insurance in a similar policy
- Other insurance in dissimilar policies

7-2. An insured's recovery from a third party (or a third party's liability insurer) could overlap with the insured's own property insurance coverage. Subrogation policy provisions allow an injured party to file a claim with his or her first-party insurer, which can then attempt to collect from the responsible third party.

7-3. Property and/or liability insurance policies may provide two or more coverages under the same policy. When these package policies are used, a given loss may be covered by more than one of the coverages offered.

▶▶

Exam Information

About Institutes Exams

Exam questions are based on the Educational Objectives stated in the course guide and textbook. The exam is designed to measure whether you have met those Educational Objectives. The exam does not test every Educational Objective. Instead, it tests over a balanced sample of Educational Objectives.

How to Prepare for Institutes Exams

What can you do to prepare for an Institutes exam? Students who pass Institute exams do the following:

- Use the assigned study materials. Focus your study on the Educational Objectives presented at the beginning of each course guide assignment. Thoroughly read the textbook and any other assigned materials, and then complete the course guide exercises. Choose a study method that best suits your needs; for example, participate in a traditional class, online class, or informal study group; or study on your own. Use the Institutes' SMART Study Aids (if available) for practice and review. If this course has an associated SMART Online Practice Exams product, you will find an access code on the inside back cover of this course guide. This access code allows you to print (in PDF format) a full practice exam and to take additional online practice exams that will simulate an actual credentialing exam.
- Become familiar with the types of test questions asked on the exam. The practice exam in this course guide or in the SMART Online Practice Exams product will help you understand the different types of questions you will encounter on the exam.
- Maximize your test-taking time. Successful students use the sample exam in the course guide or in the SMART Online Practice Exams product to practice pacing themselves. Learning how to manage your time during the exam ensures that you will complete all of the test questions in the time allotted.

Types of Exam Questions

The exam for this course consists of objective questions of several types.

The Correct-Answer Type

In this type of question, the question stem is followed by four responses, one of which is absolutely correct. Select the *correct* answer.

> Which one of the following persons evaluates requests for insurance to determine which applicants are accepted and which are rejected?
>
> a. The premium auditor
>
> b. The loss control representative
>
> c. The underwriter
>
> d. The risk manager

The Best-Answer Type

In this type of question, the question stem is followed by four responses, only one of which is best, given the statement made or facts provided in the stem. Select the *best* answer.

> Several people within an insurer might be involved in determining whether an applicant for insurance is accepted. Which one of the following positions is primarily responsible for determining whether an applicant for insurance is accepted?
>
> a. The loss control representative
>
> b. The customer service representative
>
> c. The underwriter
>
> d. The premium auditor

The Incomplete-Statement or Sentence-Completion Type

In this type of question, the last part of the question stem consists of a portion of a statement rather than a direct question. Select the phrase that *correctly* or *best* completes the sentence.

Residual market plans designed for individuals who are unable to obtain insurance on their personal property in the voluntary market are called

a. VIN plans.

b. Self-insured retention plans.

c. Premium discount plans.

d. FAIR plans.

"All of the Above" Type

In this type of question, only one of the first three answers could be correct, or all three might be correct, in which case the best answer would be "All of the above." Read all the answers and select the *best* answer.

When a large commercial insured's policy is up for renewal, who is likely to provide input to the renewal decision process?

a. The underwriter

b. The loss control representative

c. The producer

d. All of the above

"All of the following, EXCEPT:" Type

In this type of question, responses include three correct answers and one answer that is incorrect or is clearly the least correct. Select the *incorrect* or *least correct* answer.

All of the following adjust insurance claims, EXCEPT:

a. Insurer claim representatives

b. Premium auditors

c. Producers

d. Independent adjusters

About the Code of Professional Conduct

This is a brief summary of information appearing in greater detail in the CPCU Code of Professional Conduct.

All CPCU candidates and CPCUs are bound by the CPCU Code of Professional Conduct. The Code describes both high goals and minimum standards of conduct.

- The high goals described in the Canons challenge all CPCUs and CPCU candidates to aspire to the highest level of ethical performance in all of their professional activities.
- The minimum standards of conduct, described in the Rules, maintain the integrity of the CPCU designation. CPCUs and CPCU candidates are obligated to at least meet the minimum standards in the Rules, and failure to do so may subject a CPCU—or a CPCU candidate—to disciplinary measures.

In the process of satisfying the ethics requirement, CPCU candidates study the Code and are tested to ensure that all CPCUs understand their ethical obligations. The ultimate goal of the Code is to foster highly ethical conduct on the part of all CPCUs.

The CPCU Code of Professional Conduct Canons

Canon 1—Insurance professionals should endeavor to place the public interest above their own.

Canon 2—Insurance professionals should seek continually to maintain and improve their professional knowledge, skills, and competence.

Canon 3—Insurance professionals should obey all laws and regulations, and should avoid any conduct or activity that would cause unjust harm to others.

Canon 4—Insurance professionals should be diligent in the performance of their occupational duties and should continually strive to improve the functioning of the insurance mechanism.

Canon 5—Insurance professionals should **aspire to raise** the professional and ethical standards in the insurance business.

Canon 6—Insurance professionals should strive to establish and maintain dignified and honorable relationships with those whom they serve, with fellow insurance practitioners, and with members of other professions.

Canon 7—Insurance professionals should assist in improving the public understanding of insurance and risk management.

Canon 8—CPCUs should honor the integrity of the CPCU designation and respect the limitations placed on its use.

Canon 9—CPCUs should assist in maintaining the integrity of the CPCU Code of Professional Conduct.